THE

ANALECTS

Ultimate Bilingual Edition (4-in-1)

English · Traditional Chinese · Simplified Chinese · Ancient Seal Script

CONFUCIUS

CONTENTS

ABOUT THIS EDITION

Welcome to The Analects Ultimate Bilingual Edition (4-in-1). This book brings Confucius's conversations and insights to life in four parallel forms: James Legge's classic English translation, Traditional Chinese, Simplified Chinese, and Ancient Small Seal Script. Whether you're new to the Analects, exploring Chinese, or simply curious about how ideas travel across time and language, this edition invites you to read, compare, and enjoy.

The two-page spread is designed for clarity. On the left, Traditional Chinese appears above Simplified Chinese in modern left-to-right, top-to-bottom order, with punctuation added for ease. On the right, James Legge's English translation sits above the Ancient Small Seal Script. The Small Seal Script is shown in its traditional right-to-left, top-to-bottom flow and appears without punctuation.

We chose Legge's translation because it is both trustworthy and readable. Legge was among the first Western scholars to engage deeply with Classical Chinese, and his English captures the directness and dignity of the original without turning it into a puzzle. If you want a smooth first encounter with Confucius or a reliable companion for deeper reading, Legge offers both.

A quick note on history. Confucius taught in the 6th–5th centuries BCE, long before Small Seal Script was standardized under the First Emperor (Ch'in Shih-huang-ti) in 221 BCE. The Analects was first written and copied in earlier regional scripts of the late Spring and Autumn and Warring States periods. We include Small Seal here not as the handwriting of Confucius's day, but as the later, elegant standard that unified those diverse scripts. It marks the endpoint of early script evolution and shows how the writing system was eventually brought under one roof—offering a clear, beautiful counterpoint to today's Traditional and Simplified forms.

This edition keeps things simple on purpose. We present the core text without added commentary so you can meet Confucius and his students directly, in their own spare and memorable lines. The Traditional and Simplified Chinese help you see how characters are used today in different communities. The English helps you catch the meaning quickly and compare nuances. The Small Seal Script invites you to slow down, notice shapes and strokes, and appreciate the artistry of written Chinese.

We hope this four-in-one presentation offers both clarity and delight: clarity in meaning, and delight in seeing how a single thought can travel through time, script, and language without losing its spark.

學而第一

子曰：「學而時習之，不亦說乎？有朋自遠方來，不亦樂乎？人不知而不慍，不亦君子乎？」

有子曰：「其為人也孝弟，而好犯上者，鮮矣；不好犯上，而好作亂者，未之有也。君子務本，本立而道生。孝弟也者，其為仁之本與！」

子曰：「巧言令色，鮮矣仁！」

曾子曰：「吾日三省吾身：為人謀而不忠乎？與朋友交而不信乎？傳不習乎？」

子曰：「道千乘之國：敬事而信，節用而愛人，使民以時。」

学而第一

子曰：「学而时习之，不亦说乎？有朋自远方来，不亦乐乎？人不知而不愠，不亦君子乎？」

有子曰：「其为人也孝弟，而好犯上者，鲜矣；不好犯上，而好作乱者，未之有也。君子务本，本立而道生。孝弟也者，其为仁之本与！」

子曰：「巧言令色，鲜矣仁！」

曾子曰：「吾日三省吾身：为人谋而不忠乎？与朋友交而不信乎？传不习乎？」

子曰：「道千乘之国：敬事而信，节用而爱人，使民以时。」

BOOK I. HSIO R.

CHAPTER I. 1. The Master said, 'Is it not pleasant to learn with a constant perseverance and application? 2. 'Is it not delightful to have friends coming from distant quarters?' 3. 'Is he not a man of complete virtue, who feels no discomposure though men may take no note of him?'

CHAP. II. 1. The philosopher Yu said, 'They are few who, being filial and fraternal, are fond of offending against their superiors. There have been none, who, not liking to offend against their superiors, have been fond of stirring up confusion. 2. 'The superior man bends his attention to what is radical. That being established, all practical courses naturally grow up. Filial piety and fraternal submission!— are they not the root of all benevolent actions?'

CHAP. III. The Master said, 'Fine words and an insinuating appearance are seldom associated with true virtue.'

CHAP. IV. The philosopher Tsang said, 'I daily examine myself on three points:— whether, in transacting business for others, I may have been not faithful;— whether, in intercourse with friends, I may have been not sincere;— whether I may have not mastered and practised the instructions of my teacher.'

CHAP. V. The Master said, To rule a country of a thousand chariots, there must be reverent attention to business, and sincerity; economy in expenditure, and love for men; and the employment of the people at the proper seasons.'

SEAL SCRIPT

7

子曰：「弟子入則孝，出則弟，謹而信，汎愛眾，而親仁。行有餘力，則以學文。」

子夏曰：「賢賢易色，事父母能竭其力，事君能致其身，與朋友交言而有信。雖曰未學，吾必謂之學矣。」

子曰：「君子不重則不威，學則不固。主忠信，無友不如己者，過則勿憚改。」

曾子曰：「慎終追遠，民德歸厚矣。」

子曰：「弟子入则孝，出则弟，谨而信，泛爱众，而亲仁。行有余力，则以学文。」

子夏曰：「贤贤易色，事父母能竭其力，事君能致其身，与朋友交言而有信。虽曰未学，吾必谓之学矣。」

子曰：「君子不重则不威，学则不固。主忠信，无友不如己者，过则勿惮改。」

曾子曰：「慎终追远，民德归厚矣。」

CHAP. VI. The Master said, 'A youth, when at home, should be filial, and, abroad, respectful to his elders. He should be earnest and truthful. He should overflow in love to all, and cultivate the friendship of the good. When he has time and opportunity, after the performance of these things, he should employ them in polite studies.'

CHAP. VII. Tsze-hsia said, 'If a man withdraws his mind from the love of beauty, and applies it as sincerely to the love of the virtuous; if, in serving his parents, he can exert his utmost strength; if, in serving his prince, he can devote his life; if, in his intercourse with his friends, his words are sincere:— although men say that he has not learned, I will certainly say that he has.'

CHAP. VIII. 1. The Master said, 'If the scholar be not grave, he will not call forth any veneration, and his learning will not be solid. 2. 'Hold faithfulness and sincerity as first principles. 3. 'Have no friends not equal to yourself. 4. 'When you have faults, do not fear to abandon them.'

CHAP. IX. The philosopher Tsang said, 'Let there be a careful attention to perform the funeral rites to parents, and let them be followed when long gone with the ceremonies of sacrifice;— then the virtue of the people will resume its proper excellence.'

SEAL SCRIPT

9

子禽問於子貢曰：「夫子至於是邦也，必聞其政，求之與？抑與之與？」子貢曰：「夫子溫、良、恭、儉、讓以得之。夫子之求之也，其諸異乎人之求之與？」

子曰：「父在，觀其志；父沒，觀其行；三年無改於父之道，可謂孝矣。」

有子曰：「禮之用，和為貴。先王之道斯為美，小大由之。有所不行，知和而和，不以禮節之，亦不可行也。」

有子曰：「信近於義，言可復也；恭近於禮，遠恥辱也；因不失其親，亦可宗也。」

子禽问于子贡曰：「夫子至于是邦也，必闻其政，求之与？抑与之与？」子贡曰：「夫子温、良、恭、俭、让以得之。夫子之求之也，其诸异乎人之求之与？」

子曰：「父在，观其志；父没，观其行；三年无改于父之道，可谓孝矣。」

有子曰：「礼之用，和为贵。先王之道斯为美，小大由之。有所不行，知和而和，不以礼节之，亦不可行也。」

有子曰：「信近于义，言可复也；恭近于礼，远耻辱也；因不失其亲，亦可宗也。」

CHAP. X. 1. Tsze-ch'in asked Tsze-kung, saying, 'When our master comes to any country, he does not fail to learn all about its government. Does he ask his information? or is it given to him?' 2. Tsze-kung said, 'Our master is benign, upright, courteous, temperate, and complaisant, and thus he gets his information. The master's mode of asking information!— is it not different from that of other men?'

CHAP. XI. The Master said, 'While a man's father is alive, look at the bent of his will; when his father is dead, look at his conduct. If for three years he does not alter from the way of his father, he may be called filial.'

CHAP. XII. 1. The philosopher Yu said, 'In practising the rules of propriety, a natural ease is to be prized. In the ways prescribed by the ancient kings, this is the excellent quality, and in things small and great we follow them. 2. 'Yet it is not to be observed in all cases. If one, knowing how such ease should be prized, manifests it, without regulating it by the rules of propriety, this likewise is not to be done.'

CHAP. XIII. The philosopher Yu said, 'When agreements are made according to what is right, what is spoken can be made good. When respect is shown according to what is proper, one keeps far from shame and disgrace. When the parties upon whom a man leans are proper persons to be intimate with, he can make them his guides and masters.'

SEAL SCRIPT

II

子曰：「君子食無求飽，居無求安，敏於事而慎於言，就有道而正焉，可謂好學也已。」

子貢曰：「貧而無諂，富而無驕，何如？」子曰：「可也。未若貧而樂，富而好禮者也。」子貢曰：《詩》云：『如切如磋，如琢如磨。』其斯之謂與？」子曰：「賜也，始可與言詩已矣！告諸往而知來者。」

子曰：「不患人之不己知，患不知人也。」

子曰：「君子食无求饱，居无求安，敏于事而慎于言，就有道而正焉，可谓好学也已。」

子贡曰：「贫而无谄，富而无骄，何如？」子曰：「可也。未若贫而乐，富而好礼者也。」子贡曰：《诗》云：『如切如磋，如琢如磨。』其斯之谓与？」子曰：「赐也，始可与言诗已矣！告诸往而知来者。」

子曰：「不患人之不己知，患不知人也。」

CHAP. XIV. The Master said, 'He who aims to be a man of complete virtue in his food does not seek to gratify his appetite, nor in his dwelling place does he seek the appliances of ease; he is earnest in what he is doing, and careful in his speech; he frequents the company of men of principle that he may be rectified:—such a person may be said indeed to love to learn.'

CHAP. XV. 1. Tsze-kung said, 'What do you pronounce concerning the poor man who yet does not flatter, and the rich man who is not proud?' The Master replied, 'They will do; but they are not equal to him, who, though poor, is yet cheerful, and to him, who, though rich, loves the rules of propriety.' 2. Tsze-kung replied, 'It is said in the Book of Poetry, "As you cut and then file, as you carve and then polish."— The meaning is the same, I apprehend, as that which you have just expressed.' 3. The Master said, 'With one like Ts'ze, I can begin to talk about the odes. I told him one point, and he knew its proper sequence.'

CHAP. XVI. The Master said, 'I will not be afflicted at men's not knowing me; I will be afflicted that I do not know men.'

SEAL SCRIPT

為政第二

子曰：「為政以德，譬如北辰，居其所而眾星共之。」

子曰：「詩三百，一言以蔽之，曰『思無邪』。」

子曰：「道之以政，齊之以刑，民免而無恥；道之以德，齊之以禮，有恥且格。」

子曰：「吾十有五而志于學，三十而立，四十而不惑，五十而知天命，六十而耳順，七十而從心所欲，不踰矩。」

为政第二

子曰：「为政以德，譬如北辰，居其所而众星共之。」

子曰：「诗三百，一言以蔽之，曰『思无邪』。」

子曰：「道之以政，齐之以刑，民免而无耻；道之以德，齐之以礼，有耻且格。」

子曰：「吾十有五而志于学，三十而立，四十而不惑，五十而知天命，六十而耳顺，七十而从心所欲，不逾矩。」

BOOK II. WEI CHANG.

CHAP. I. The Master said, 'He who exercises government by means of his virtue may be compared to the north polar star, which keeps its place and all the stars turn towards it.'

CHAP. II. The Master said, 'In the Book of Poetry are three hundred pieces, but the design of them all may be embraced in one sentence— "Having no depraved thoughts."'

CHAP. III. 1. The Master said, 'If the people be led by laws, and uniformity sought to be given them by punishments, they will try to avoid the punishment, but have no sense of shame. 2. 'If they be led by virtue, and uniformity sought to be given them by the rules of propriety, they will have the sense of shame, and moreover will become good.'

CHAP. IV. 1. The Master said, 'At fifteen, I had my mind bent on learning. 2. 'At thirty, I stood firm. 3. 'At forty, I had no doubts. 4. 'At fifty, I knew the decrees of Heaven. 5. 'At sixty, my ear was an obedient organ for the reception of truth. 6. 'At seventy, I could follow what my heart desired, without transgressing what was right.'

SEAL SCRIPT

　　孟懿子問孝。子曰：「無違。」樊遲御，子告之曰：「孟孫問
孝於我，我對曰『無違』。」樊遲曰：「何謂也？」子曰：「生事
之以禮；死葬之以禮，祭之以禮。」

　　孟武伯問孝。子曰：「父母唯其疾之憂。」

　　子游問孝。子曰：「今之孝者，是謂能養。至於犬馬，皆能
有養；不敬，何以別乎？」

　　子夏問孝。子曰：「色難。有事弟子服其勞，有酒食先生饌，
曾是以為孝乎？」

　　孟懿子问孝。子曰：「无违。」樊迟御，子告之曰：「孟孙问
孝于我，我对曰『无违』。」樊迟曰：「何谓也？」子曰：「生事
之以礼；死葬之以礼，祭之以礼。」

　　孟武伯问孝。子曰：「父母唯其疾之忧。」

　　子游问孝。子曰：「今之孝者，是谓能养。至于犬马，皆能
有养；不敬，何以别乎？」

　　子夏问孝。子曰：「色难。有事弟子服其劳，有酒食先生馔，
曾是以为孝乎？」

CHAP. V. 1. Mang I asked what filial piety was. The Master said, 'It is not being disobedient.' 2. Soon after, as Fan Ch'ih was driving him, the Master told him, saying, 'Mang-sun asked me what filial piety was, and I answered him,— "not being disobedient."' 3. Fan Ch'ih said, 'What did you mean?' The Master replied, 'That parents, when alive, be served according to propriety; that, when dead, they should be buried according to propriety; and that they should be sacrificed to according to propriety.'

CHAP. VI. Mang Wu asked what filial piety was. The Master said, 'Parents are anxious lest their children should be sick.'

CHAP. VII. Tsze-yu asked what filial piety was. The Master said, 'The filial piety of now-a-days means the support of one's parents. But dogs and horses likewise are able to do something in the way of support;— without reverence, what is there to distinguish the one support given from the other?'

CHAP. VIII. Tsze-hsia asked what filial piety was. The Master said, 'The difficulty is with the countenance. If, when their elders have any troublesome affairs, the young take the toil of them, and if, when the young have wine and food, they set them before their elders, is THIS to be considered filial piety?'

SEAL SCRIPT

　　子曰：「吾與回言終日，不違如愚。退而省其私，亦足以發。回也，不愚。」

　　子曰：「視其所以，觀其所由，察其所安。人焉廋哉？人焉廋哉？」

　　子曰：「溫故而知新，可以為師矣。」

　　子曰：「君子不器。」

　　子貢問君子。子曰：「先行其言，而後從之。」

　　子曰：「君子周而不比，小人比而不周。」

　　子曰：「吾与回言终日，不违如愚。退而省其私，亦足以发。回也，不愚。」

　　子曰：「视其所以，观其所由，察其所安。人焉廋哉？人焉廋哉？」

　　子曰：「温故而知新，可以为师矣。」

　　子曰：「君子不器。」

　　子贡问君子。子曰：「先行其言，而后从之。」

　　子曰：「君子周而不比，小人比而不周。」

CHAP. IX. The Master said, 'I have talked with Hui for a whole day, and he has not made any objection to anything I said;— as if he were stupid. He has retired, and I have examined his conduct when away from me, and found him able to illustrate my teachings. Hui!— He is not stupid.'

CHAP. X. 1. The Master said, 'See what a man does. 2. 'Mark his motives. 3. 'Examine in what things he rests. 4. 'How can a man conceal his character? 5. How can a man conceal his character?'

CHAP. XI. The Master said, 'If a man keeps cherishing his old knowledge, so as continually to be acquiring new, he may be a teacher of others.'

CHAP. XII. The Master said, 'The accomplished scholar is not a utensil.'

CHAP. XIII. Tsze-kung asked what constituted the superior man. The Master said, 'He acts before he speaks, and afterwards speaks according to his actions.'

CHAP. XIV. The Master said, 'The superior man is catholic and no partisan. The mean man is partisan and not catholic.'

SEAL SCRIPT

　　子曰：「學而不思則罔，思而不學則殆。」

　　子曰：「攻乎異端，斯害也已！」

　　子曰：「由！誨女知之乎？知之為知之，不知為不知，是知也。」

　　子張學干祿。子曰：「多聞闕疑，慎言其餘，則寡尤；多見闕殆，慎行其餘，則寡悔。言寡尤，行寡悔，祿在其中矣。」

　　哀公問曰：「何為則民服？」孔子對曰：「舉直錯諸枉，則民服；舉枉錯諸直，則民不服。」

　　子曰：「学而不思则罔，思而不学则殆。」

　　子曰：「攻乎异端，斯害也已！」

　　子曰：「由！诲女知之乎？知之为知之，不知为不知，是知也。」

　　子张学干禄。子曰：「多闻阙疑，慎言其余，则寡尤；多见阙殆，慎行其余，则寡悔。言寡尤，行寡悔，禄在其中矣。」

　　哀公问曰：「何为则民服？」孔子对曰：「举直错诸枉，则民服；举枉错诸直，则民不服。」

CHAP. XV. The Master said, 'Learning without thought is labour lost; thought without learning is perilous.'

CHAP. XVI. The Master said, 'The study of strange doctrines is injurious indeed!'

CHAP. XVII. The Master said, 'Yu, shall I teach you what knowledge is? When you know a thing, to hold that you know it; and when you do not know a thing, to allow that you do not know it;— this is knowledge.'

CHAP. XVII. 1. Tsze-chang was learning with a view to official emolument. 2. The Master said, 'Hear much and put aside the points of which you stand in doubt, while you speak cautiously at the same time of the others:— then you will afford few occasions for blame. See much and put aside the things which seem perilous, while you are cautious at the same time in carrying the others into practice:— then you will have few occasions for repentance. When one gives few occasions for blame in his words, and few occasions for repentance in his con-duct, he is in the way to get emolument.'

CHAP. XIX. The Duke Ai asked, saying, 'What should be done in order to secure the submission of the people?' Confucius replied, 'Advance the upright and set aside the crooked, then the people will submit. Advance the crooked and set aside the upright, then the people will not submit.'

SEAL SCRIPT

季康子問：「使民敬、忠以勸，如之何？」子曰：「臨之以莊則敬，孝慈則忠，舉善而教不能，則勸。」

或謂孔子曰：「子奚不為政？」子曰：「《書》云：『孝乎惟孝、友于兄弟，施於有政。』是亦為政，奚其為為政？」

子曰：「人而無信，不知其可也。 大車無輗，小車無軏，其何以行之哉？」

季康子问：「使民敬、忠以劝，如之何？」子曰：「临之以庄则敬，孝慈则忠，举善而教不能，则劝。」

或谓孔子曰：「子奚不为政？」子曰：「《书》云：『孝乎惟孝、友于兄弟，施于有政。』是亦为政，奚其为为政？」

子曰：「人而无信，不知其可也。大车无輗，小车无軏，其何以行之哉？」

CHAP. XX. Chi K'ang asked how to cause the people to reverence their ruler, to be faithful to him, and to go on to nerve themselves to virtue. The Master said, 'Let him preside over them with gravity;— then they will reverence him. Let him be filial and kind to all;— then they will be faithful to him. Let him advance the good and teach the incompetent;— then they will eagerly seek to be virtuous.'

CHAP. XXI. 1. Some one addressed Confucius, saying, 'Sir, why are you not engaged in the government?' 2. The Master said, 'What does the Shu-ching say of filial piety?— "You are filial, you discharge your brotherly duties. These qualities are displayed in government." This then also constitutes the exercise of government. Why must there be THAT— making one be in the government?'

CHAP. XXII. The Master said, 'I do not know how a man without truthfulness is to get on. How can a large carriage be made to go without the cross-bar for yoking the oxen to, or a small carriage without the arrangement for yoking the horses?'

SEAL SCRIPT

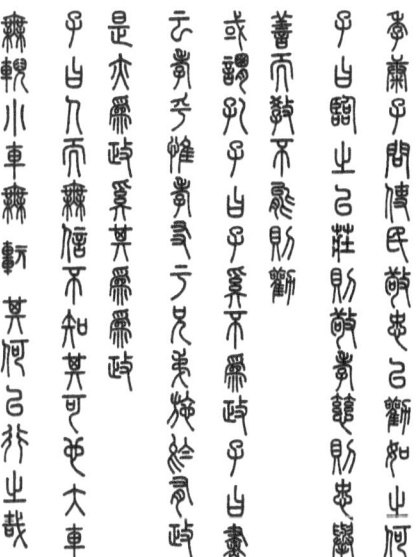

　　子張問：「十世可知也？」子曰：「殷因於夏禮，所損益，可知也；周因於殷禮，所損益，可知也；其或繼周者，雖百世可知也。」

　　子曰：「非其鬼而祭之，諂也。見義不為，無勇也。」

　　子张问：「十世可知也？」子曰：「殷因于夏礼，所损益，可知也；周因于殷礼，所损益，可知也；其或继周者，虽百世可知也。」

　　子曰：「非其鬼而祭之，谄也。见义不为，无勇也。」

CHAP. XXIII. 1. Tsze-chang asked whether the affairs of ten ages after could be known. 2. Confucius said, 'The Yin dynasty followed the regulations of the Hsia: wherein it took from or added to them may be known. The Chau dynasty has followed the regulations of Yin: wherein it took from or added to them may be known. Some other may follow the Chau, but though it should be at the distance of a hundred ages, its affairs may be known.'

CHAP. XXIV. 1. The Master said, 'For a man to sacrifice to a spirit which does not belong to him is flattery. 2. 'To see what is right and not to do it is want of courage.'

SEAL SCRIPT

八佾第三

孔子謂季氏：「八佾舞於庭，是可忍也，孰不可忍也？」

三家者以雍徹。子曰：「『相維辟公，天子穆穆』，奚取於三家之堂？」

子曰：「人而不仁，如禮何？人而不仁，如樂何？」

林放問禮之本。子曰：「大哉問！禮，與其奢也，寧儉；喪，與其易也，寧戚。」

子曰：「夷狄之有君，不如諸夏之亡也。」

八佾第三

孔子谓季氏：「八佾舞于庭，是可忍也，孰不可忍也？」

三家者以雍彻。子曰：「『相维辟公，天子穆穆』，奚取于三家之堂？」

子曰：「人而不仁，如礼何？人而不仁，如乐何？」

林放问礼之本。子曰：「大哉问！礼，与其奢也，宁俭；丧，与其易也，宁戚。」

子曰：「夷狄之有君，不如诸夏之亡也。」

BOOK III. PA YIH.

CHAP. I. Confucius said of the head of the Chi family, who had eight rows of pantomimes in his area, 'If he can bear to do this, what may he not bear to do?'

CHAP. II. The three families used the YUNG ode, while the vessels were being removed, at the conclusion of the sacrifice. The Master said, '"Assisting are the princes;— the son of heaven looks profound and grave:"— what application can these words have in the hall of the three families?'

CHAP. III. The Master said, 'If a man be without the virtues proper to humanity, what has he to do with the rites of propriety? If a man be without the virtues proper to humanity, what has he to do with music?'

CHAP. IV. 1. Lin Fang asked what was the first thing to be attended to in ceremonies. 2. The Master said, 'A great question indeed! 3. 'In festive ceremonies, it is better to be sparing than extravagant. In the ceremonies of mourning, it is better that there be deep sorrow than a minute attention to observances.'

CHAP. V. The Master said, 'The rude tribes of the east and north have their princes, and are not like the States of our great land which are without them.'

SEAL SCRIPT

　　季氏旅於泰山。子謂冉有曰：「女弗能救與？」對曰：「不能。」
子曰：「嗚呼！曾謂泰山，不如林放乎？」
　　子曰：「君子無所爭，必也射乎！揖讓而升，下而飲，其爭
也君子。」
　　子夏問曰：「『巧笑倩兮，美目盼兮，素以為絢兮。』何謂也？」
子曰：「繪事後素。」曰：「禮後乎？」子曰：「起予者商也！始
可與言詩已矣。」
　　子曰：「夏禮，吾能言之，杞不足徵也；殷禮，吾能言之，
宋不足徵也。文獻不足故也，足則吾能徵之矣。」

　　季氏旅于泰山。子谓冉有曰：「女弗能救与？」对曰：「不能。」
子曰：「呜呼！曾谓泰山，不如林放乎？」
　　子曰：「君子无所争，必也射乎！揖让而升，下而饮，其争
也君子。」
　　子夏问曰：「『巧笑倩兮，美目盼兮，素以为绚兮。』何谓也？」
子曰：「绘事后素。」曰：「礼后乎？」子曰：「起予者商也！始
可与言诗已矣。」
　　子曰：「夏礼，吾能言之，杞不足征也；殷礼，吾能言之，
宋不足征也。文献不足故也，足则吾能征之矣。」

CHAP. VI. The chief of the Chi family was about to sacrifice to the T'ai mountain. The Master said to Zan Yu, 'Can you not save him from this?' He answered, 'I cannot.' Confucius said, 'Alas! will you say that the T'ai mountain is not so discerning as Lin Fang?'

CHAP. VII. The Master said, 'The student of virtue has no contentions. If it be said he cannot avoid them, shall this be in archery? But he bows complaisantly to his competitors; thus he ascends the hall, descends, and exacts the forfeit of drinking. In his contention, he is still the Chun-tsze.'

CHAP. VIII. 1. Tsze-hsia asked, saying, 'What is the meaning of the passage— "The pretty dimples of her artful smile! The well- defined black and white of her eye! The plain ground for the colours?"' 2. The Master said, 'The business of laying on the colours follows (the preparation of) the plain ground.' 3. 'Ceremonies then are a subsequent thing?' The Master said, 'It is Shang who can bring out my meaning. Now I can begin to talk about the odes with him.'

CHAP. IX. The Master said, 'I could describe the ceremonies of the Hsia dynasty, but Chi cannot sufficiently attest my words. I could describe the ceremonies of the Yin dynasty, but Sung cannot sufficiently attest my words. (They cannot do so) because of the insufficiency of their records and wise men. If those were sufficient, I could adduce them in support of my words.'

SEAL SCRIPT

子曰：「禘自既灌而往者，吾不欲觀之矣。」

或問禘之說。子曰：「不知也。知其說者之於天下也，其如示諸斯乎！」指其掌。

祭如在，祭神如神在。子曰：「吾不與祭，如不祭。」

王孫賈問曰：「與其媚於奧，寧媚於竈，何謂也？」子曰：「不然，獲罪於天，無所禱也。」

子曰：「周監於二代，郁郁乎文哉！吾從周。」

子入大廟，每事問。或曰：「孰謂鄹人之子知禮乎？入大廟，每事問。」子聞之曰：「是禮也。」

子曰：「禘自既灌而往者，吾不欲观之矣。」

或问禘之说。子曰：「不知也。知其说者之于天下也，其如示诸斯乎！」指其掌。

祭如在，祭神如神在。子曰：「吾不与祭，如不祭。」

王孙贾问曰：「与其媚于奥，宁媚于灶，何谓也？」子曰：「不然，获罪于天，无所祷也。」

子曰：「周监于二代，郁郁乎文哉！吾从周。」

子入大庙，每事问。或曰：「孰谓鄹人之子知礼乎？入大庙，每事问。」子闻之曰：「是礼也。」

CHAP. X. The Master said, 'At the great sacrifice, after the pouring out of the libation, I have no wish to look on.'

CHAP. XI. Some one asked the meaning of the great sacrifice. The Master said, 'I do not know. He who knew its meaning would find it as easy to govern the kingdom as to look on this;— pointing to his palm.

CHAP. XII. 1. He sacrificed to the dead, as if they were present. He sacrificed to the spirits, as if the spirits were present. 2. The Master said, 'I consider my not being present at the sacrifice, as if I did not sacrifice.'

CHAP. XIII. 1. Wang-sun Chia asked, saying, 'What is the meaning of the saying, "It is better to pay court to the furnace than to the south-west corner?"' 2. The Master said, 'Not so. He who offends against Heaven has none to whom he can pray.'

CHAP. XIV. The Master said, 'Chau had the advantage of viewing the two past dynasties. How complete and elegant are its regulations! I follow Chau.'

CHAP. XV. The Master, when he entered the grand temple, asked about everything. Some one said, 'Who will say that the son of the man of Tsau knows the rules of propriety! He has entered the grand temple and asks about everything.' The Master heard the remark, and said, 'This is a rule of propriety.'

SEAL SCRIPT

31

子曰：「射不主皮，為力不同科，古之道也。」

子貢欲去告朔之餼羊。子曰：「賜也，爾愛其羊，我愛其禮。」

子曰：「事君盡禮，人以為諂也。」

定公問：「君使臣，臣事君，如之何？」孔子對曰：「君使臣以禮，臣事君以忠。」

子曰：「關雎，樂而不淫，哀而不傷。」

子曰：「射不主皮，为力不同科，古之道也。」

子贡欲去告朔之饩羊。子曰：「赐也，尔爱其羊，我爱其礼。」

子曰：「事君尽礼，人以为谄也。」

定公问：「君使臣，臣事君，如之何？」孔子对曰：「君使臣以礼，臣事君以忠。」

子曰：「关雎，乐而不淫，哀而不伤。」

CHAP. XVI. The Master said, 'In archery it is not going through the leather which is the principal thing;— because people's strength is not equal. This was the old way.'

CHAP. XVII. 1. Tsze-kung wished to do away with the offering of a sheep connected with the inauguration of the first day of each month. 2. The Master said, 'Ts'ze, you love the sheep; I love the ceremony.'

CHAP. XVII. The Master said, 'The full observance of the rules of propriety in serving one's prince is accounted by people to be flattery.'

CHAP. XIX. The Duke Ting asked how a prince should employ his ministers, and how ministers should serve their prince. Confucius replied, 'A prince should employ his minister according to according to the rules of propriety; ministers should serve their prince with faithfulness.'

CHAP. XX. The Master said, 'The Kwan Tsu is expressive of enjoyment without being licentious, and of grief without being hurtfully excessive.'

SEAL SCRIPT

　　哀公問社於宰我。宰我對曰：「夏后氏以松，殷人以柏，周人以栗，曰使民戰栗。」子聞之曰：「成事不說，遂事不諫，既往不咎。」

　　子曰：「管仲之器小哉！」或曰：「管仲儉乎？」曰：「管氏有三歸，官事不攝，焉得儉？」「然則管仲知禮乎？」曰：「邦君樹塞門，管氏亦樹塞門；邦君為兩君之好，有反坫，管氏亦有反坫。管氏而知禮，孰不知禮？」

　　哀公问社于宰我。宰我对曰：「夏后氏以松，殷人以柏，周人以栗，曰使民战栗。」子闻之曰：「成事不说，遂事不谏，既往不咎。」

　　子曰：「管仲之器小哉！」或曰：「管仲俭乎？」曰：「管氏有三归，官事不摄，焉得俭？」「然则管仲知礼乎？」曰：「邦君树塞门，管氏亦树塞门；邦君为两君之好，有反坫，管氏亦有反坫。管氏而知礼，孰不知礼？」

CHAP. XXI. 1. The Duke Ai asked Tsai Wo about the altars of the spirits of the land. Tsai Wo replied, 'The Hsia sovereign planted the pine tree about them; the men of the Yin planted the cypress; and the men of the Chau planted the chestnut tree, meaning thereby to cause the people to be in awe.' 2. When the Master heard it, he said, 'Things that are done, it is needless to speak about; things that have had their course, it is needless to remonstrate about; things that are past, it is needless to blame.'

CHAP. XXII. 1. The Master said, 'Small indeed was the capacity of Kwan Chung!' 2. Some one said, 'Was Kwan Chung parsimonious?' 'Kwan,' was the reply, 'had the San Kwei, and his officers performed no double duties; how can he be considered parsimonious?' 3. 'Then, did Kwan Chung know the rules of propriety?' The Master said, 'The princes of States have a screen intercepting the view at their gates. Kwan had likewise a screen at his gate. The princes of States on any friendly meeting between two of them, had a stand on which to place their inverted cups. Kwan had also such a stand. If Kwan knew the rules of propriety, who does not know them?'

SEAL SCRIPT

35

子語魯大師樂。曰：「樂其可知也：始作，翕如也；從之，純如也，皦如也，繹如也，以成。」

儀封人請見。曰：「君子之至於斯也，吾未嘗不得見也。」從者見之。出曰：「二三子，何患於喪乎？天下之無道也久矣，天將以夫子為木鐸。」

子謂韶，「盡美矣，又盡善也。」謂武，「盡美矣，未盡善也」。

子曰：「居上不寬，為禮不敬，臨喪不哀，吾何以觀之哉？」

子语鲁大师乐。曰：「乐其可知也：始作，翕如也；从之，纯如也，皦如也，绎如也，以成。」

仪封人请见。曰：「君子之至于斯也，吾未尝不得见也。」从者见之。出曰：「二三子，何患于丧乎？天下之无道也久矣，天将以夫子为木铎。」

子谓韶，「尽美矣，又尽善也。」谓武，「尽美矣，未尽善也」。

子曰：「居上不宽，为礼不敬，临丧不哀，吾何以观之哉？」

CHAP. XXXII. The Master instructing the grand music-master of Lu said, 'How to play music may be known. At the commencement of the piece, all the parts should sound together. As it proceeds, they should be in harmony while severally distinct and flowing without break, and thus on to the conclusion.'

CHAP. XXIV. The border warden at Yi requested to be introduced to the Master, saying, 'When men of superior virtue have come to this, I have never been denied the privilege of seeing them.' The followers of the sage introduced him, and when he came out from the interview, he said, 'My friends, why are you distressed by your master's loss of office? The kingdom has long been without the principles of truth and right; Heaven is going to use your master as a bell with its wooden tongue.'

CHAP. XXV. The Master said of the Shao that it was perfectly beautiful and also perfectly good. He said of the Wu that it was perfectly beautiful but not perfectly good.

CHAP. XXVI. The Master said, 'High station filled without indulgent generosity; ceremonies performed without reverence; mourning conducted without sorrow;— wherewith should I contemplate such ways?'

SEAL SCRIPT

里仁第四

子曰：「里仁為美。擇不處仁，焉得知？」

子曰：「不仁者不可以久處約，不可以長處樂。仁者安仁，知者利仁。」

子曰：「唯仁者能好人，能惡人。」

子曰：「苟志於仁矣，無惡也。」

子曰：「富與貴是人之所欲也，不以其道得之，不處也；貧與賤是人之所惡也，不以其道得之，不去也。君子去仁，惡乎成名？君子無終食之間違仁，造次必於是，顛沛必於是。」

SIMPLIFIED CHINESE

里仁第四

子曰：「里仁为美。择不处仁，焉得知？」

子曰：「不仁者不可以久处约，不可以长处乐。仁者安仁，知者利仁。」

子曰：「唯仁者能好人，能恶人。」

子曰：「苟志于仁矣，无恶也。」

子曰：「富与贵是人之所欲也，不以其道得之，不处也；贫与贱是人之所恶也，不以其道得之，不去也。君子去仁，恶乎成名？君子无终食之间违仁，造次必于是，颠沛必于是。」

BOOK IV. LE JIN.

CHAP. I. The Master said, 'It is virtuous manners which constitute the excellence of a neighborhood. If a man in selecting a residence, do not fix on one where such prevail, how can he be wise?'

CHAP. II. The Master said, 'Those who are without virtue cannot abide long either in a condition of poverty and hardship, or in a condition of enjoyment. The virtuous rest in virtue; the wise desire virtue.'

CHAP. III. The Master said, 'It is only the (truly) virtuous man, who can love, or who can hate, others.'

CHAP. IV. The Master said, 'If the will be set on virtue, there will be no practice of wickedness.'

CHAP. V. 1. The Master said, 'Riches and honours are what men desire. If it cannot be obtained in the proper way, they should not be held. Poverty and meanness are what men dislike. If it cannot be avoided in the proper way, they should not be avoided. 2. 'If a superior man abandon virtue, how can he fulfil the requirements of that name? 3. 'The superior man does not, even for the space of a single meal, act contrary to virtue. In moments of haste, he cleaves to it. In seasons of danger, he cleaves to it.'

SEAL SCRIPT

子曰：「我未見好仁者，惡不仁者。好仁者，無以尚之；惡不仁者，其為仁矣，不使不仁者加乎其身。有能一日用其力於仁矣乎？我未見力不足者。蓋有之矣，我未之見也。」

子曰：「人之過也，各於其黨。觀過，斯知仁矣。」

子曰：「朝聞道，夕死可矣。」

子曰：「士志於道，而恥惡衣惡食者，未足與議也。」

子曰：「君子之於天下也，無適也，無莫也，義之與比。」

子曰：「君子懷德，小人懷土；君子懷刑，小人懷惠。」

子曰：「我未见好仁者，恶不仁者。好仁者，无以尚之；恶不仁者，其为仁矣，不使不仁者加乎其身。有能一日用其力于仁矣乎？我未见力不足者。盖有之矣，我未之见也。」

子曰：「人之过也，各于其党。观过，斯知仁矣。」

子曰：「朝闻道，夕死可矣。」

子曰：「士志于道，而耻恶衣恶食者，未足与议也。」

子曰：「君子之于天下也，无适也，无莫也，义之与比。」

子曰：「君子怀德，小人怀土；君子怀刑，小人怀惠。」

CHAP. VI. 1. The Master said, 'I have not seen a person who loved virtue, or one who hated what was not virtuous. He who loved virtue, would esteem nothing above it. He who hated what is not virtuous, would practise virtue in such a way that he would not allow anything that is not virtuous to approach his person. 2. 'Is any one able for one day to apply his strength to virtue? I have not seen the case in which his strength would be insufficient. 3. 'Should there possibly be any such case, I have not seen it.'

CHAP. VII. The Master said, 'The faults of men are characteristic of the class to which they belong. By observing a man's faults, it may be known that he is virtuous.'

CHAP. VIII. The Master said, 'If a man in the morning hear the right way, he may die in the evening without regret.'

CHAP. IX. The Master said, 'A scholar, whose mind is set on truth, and who is ashamed of bad clothes and bad food, is not fit to be discoursed with.'

CHAP. X. The Master said, 'The superior man, in the world, does not set his mind either for anything, or against anything; what is right he will follow.'

CHAP. XI. The Master said, 'The superior man thinks of virtue; the small man thinks of comfort. The superior man thinks of the sanctions of law; the small man thinks of favours which he may receive.'

SEAL SCRIPT

41

　　子曰：「放於利而行，多怨。」

　　子曰：「能以禮讓為國乎？何有？不能以禮讓為國，如禮
何？」

　　子曰：「不患無位，患所以立；不患莫己知，求為可知也。」

　　子曰：「參乎！吾道一以貫之。」曾子曰：「唯。」子出。門
人問曰：「何謂也？」曾子曰：「夫子之道，忠恕而已矣。」

　　子曰：「君子喻於義，小人喻於利。」

　　子曰：「見賢思齊焉，見不賢而內自省也。」

　　子曰：「放于利而行，多怨。」

　　子曰：「能以礼让为国乎？何有？不能以礼让为国，如礼
何？」

　　子曰：「不患无位，患所以立；不患莫己知，求为可知也。」

　　子曰：「参乎！吾道一以贯之。」曾子曰：「唯。」子出。门
人问曰：「何谓也？」曾子曰：「夫子之道，忠恕而已矣。」

　　子曰：「君子喻于义，小人喻于利。」

　　子曰：「见贤思齐焉，见不贤而内自省也。」

CHAP. XII. The Master said: 'He who acts with a constant view to his own advantage will be much murmured against.'

CHAP. XIII. The Master said, 'If a prince is able to govern his kingdom with the complaisance proper to the rules of propriety, what difficulty will he have? If he cannot govern it with that complaisance, what has he to do with the rules of propriety?'

CHAP. XIV. The Master said, 'A man should say, I am not concerned that I have no place, I am concerned how I may fit myself for one. I am not concerned that I am not known, I seek to be worthy to be known.'

CHAP. XV. 1. The Master said, 'Shan, my doctrine is that of an all-pervading unity.' The disciple Tsang replied, 'Yes.' 2. The Master went out, and the other disciples asked, saying, 'What do his words mean?' Tsang said, 'The doctrine of our master is to be true to the principles of our nature and the benevolent exercise of them to others,— this and nothing more.'

CHAP. XVI. The Master said, 'The mind of the superior man is conversant with righteousness; the mind of the mean man is conversant with gain.'

CHAP. XVII. The Master said, 'When we see men of worth, we should think of equalling them; when we see men of a contrary character, we should turn inwards and examine ourselves.'

SEAL SCRIPT

子曰：「事父母幾諫。見志不從，又敬不違，勞而不怨。」
子曰：「父母在，不遠遊。遊必有方。」
子曰：「三年無改於父之道，可謂孝矣。」
子曰：「父母之年，不可不知也。一則以喜，一則以懼。」
子曰：「古者言之不出，恥躬之不逮也。」

子曰：「事父母几谏。见志不从，又敬不违，劳而不怨。」
子曰：「父母在，不远游。游必有方。」
子曰：「三年无改于父之道，可谓孝矣。」
子曰：「父母之年，不可不知也。一则以喜，一则以惧。」
子曰：「古者言之不出，恥躬之不逮也。」

CHAP. XVIII. The Master said, 'In serving his parents, a son may remonstrate with them, but gently; when he sees that they do not incline to follow his advice, he shows an increased degree of reverence, but does not abandon his purpose; and should they punish him, he does not allow himself to murmur.'

CHAP. XIX. The Master said, 'While his parents are alive, the son may not go abroad to a distance. If he does go abroad, he must have a fixed place to which he goes.'

CHAP. XX. The Master said, 'If the son for three years does not alter from the way of his father, he may be called filial.'

CHAP. XXI. The Master said, 'The years of parents may by no means not be kept in the memory, as an occasion at once for joy and for fear.'

CHAP. XXII. The Master said, 'The reason why the ancients did not readily give utterance to their words, was that they feared lest their actions should not come up to them.'

SEAL SCRIPT

子曰：「以約失之者，鮮矣。」
子曰：「君子欲訥於言，而敏於行。」
子曰：「德不孤，必有鄰。」
子游曰：「事君數，斯辱矣，朋友數，斯疏矣。」

子曰：「以约失之者，鲜矣。」
子曰：「君子欲讷于言，而敏于行。」
子曰：「德不孤，必有邻。」
子游曰：「事君数，斯辱矣，朋友数，斯疏矣。」

CHAP. XXIII. The Master said, 'The cautious seldom err.'

CHAP. XXIV. The Master said, 'The superior man wishes to be slow in his speech and earnest in his conduct.'

CHAP. XXV. The Master said, 'Virtue is not left to stand alone. He who practises it will have neighbors.'

CHAP. XXVI. Tsze-yu said, 'In serving a prince, frequent remonstrances lead to disgrace. Between friends, frequent reproofs make the friendship distant.'

SEAL SCRIPT

公冶長第五

子謂公冶長，「可妻也。雖在縲絏之中，非其罪也」。以其子妻之。

子謂南容，「邦有道，不廢；邦無道，免於刑戮。」以其兄之子妻之。

子謂子賤，「君子哉若人！魯無君子者，斯焉取斯？」

子貢問曰：「賜也何如？」子曰：「女器也。」曰：「何器也？」曰：「瑚璉也。」

或曰：「雍也，仁而不佞。」子曰：「焉用佞？禦人以口給，屢憎於人。不知其仁，焉用佞？」

公冶长第五

子谓公冶长，「可妻也。虽在缧绁之中，非其罪也」。以其子妻之。

子谓南容，「邦有道，不废；邦无道，免于刑戮。」以其兄之子妻之。

子谓子贱，「君子哉若人！鲁无君子者，斯焉取斯？」

子贡问曰：「赐也何如？」子曰：「女器也。」曰：「何器也？」曰：「瑚琏也。」

或曰：「雍也，仁而不佞。」子曰：「焉用佞？御人以口给，屡憎于人。不知其仁，焉用佞？」

BOOK V. KUNG-YE CH'ANG.

CHAP. I. 1. The Master said of Kung-ye Ch'ang that he might be wived; although he was put in bonds, he had not been guilty of any crime. Accordingly, he gave him his own daughter to wife. 2. Of Nan Yung he said that if the country were well governed he would not be out of office, and if it were ill-governed, he would escape punishment and disgrace. He gave him the daughter of his own elder brother to wife.

CHAP. II. The Master said of Tsze-chien, 'Of superior virtue indeed is such a man! If there were not virtuous men in Lu, how could this man have acquired this character?'

CHAP. III. Tsze-kung asked, 'What do you say of me, Ts'ze? The Master said, 'You are a utensil.' 'What utensil?' 'A gemmed sacrificial utensil.'

CHAP. IV. 1. Some one said, 'Yung is truly virtuous, but he is not ready with his tongue.' 2. The Master said, 'What is the good of being ready with the tongue? They who encounter men with smartnesses of speech for the most part procure themselves hatred. I know not whether he be truly virtuous, but why should he show readiness of the tongue?'

SEAL SCRIPT

49

子使漆雕開仕。對曰：「吾斯之未能信。」子說。

子曰：「道不行，乘桴浮于海。從我者其由與？」子路聞之喜。子曰：「由也好勇過我，無所取材。」

孟武伯問：「子路仁乎？」子曰：「不知也。」又問。子曰：「由也，千乘之國，可使治其賦也，不知其仁也。」「求也何如？」子曰：「求也，千室之邑，百乘之家，可使為之宰也，不知其仁也。」「赤也何如？」子曰：「赤也，束帶立於朝，可使與賓客言也，不知其仁也。」

子使漆雕开仕。对曰：「吾斯之未能信。」子说。

子曰：「道不行，乘桴浮于海。从我者其由与？」子路闻之喜。子曰：「由也好勇过我，无所取材。」

孟武伯问：「子路仁乎？」子曰：「不知也。」又问。子曰：「由也，千乘之国，可使治其赋也，不知其仁也。」「求也何如？」子曰：「求也，千室之邑，百乘之家，可使为之宰也，不知其仁也。」「赤也何如？」子曰：「赤也，束带立于朝，可使与宾客言也，不知其仁也。」

CHAP. V. The Master was wishing Ch'i-tiao K'ai to enter on official employment. He replied, 'I am not yet able to rest in the assurance of THIS.' The Master was pleased.

CHAP. VI. The Master said, 'My doctrines make no way. I will get upon a raft, and float about on the sea. He that will accompany me will be Yu, I dare say.' Tsze-lu hearing this was glad, upon which the Master said, 'Yu is fonder of daring than I am. He does not exercise his judgment upon matters.'

CHAP. VII. 1. Mang Wu asked about Tsze-lu, whether he was perfectly virtuous. The Master said, 'I do not know.' 2. He asked again, when the Master replied, 'In a kingdom of a thousand chariots, Yu might be employed to manage the military levies, but I do not know whether he be perfectly virtuous.' 3. 'And what do you say of Ch'iu?' The Master replied, 'In a city of a thousand families, or a clan of a hundred chariots, Ch'iu might be employed as governor, but I do not know whether he is perfectly virtuous.' 4. 'What do you say of Ch'ih?' The Master replied, 'With his sash girt and standing in a court, Ch'ih might be employed to converse with the visitors and guests, but I do not know whether he is perfectly virtuous.'

SEAL SCRIPT

子謂子貢曰：「女與回也孰愈？」對曰：「賜也何敢望回。回也聞一以知十，賜也聞一以知二。」子曰：「弗如也！吾與女弗如也。」

宰予晝寢。子曰：「朽木不可雕也，糞土之牆不可杇也，於予與何誅。」子曰：「始吾於人也，聽其言而信其行；今吾於人也，聽其言而觀其行。於予與改是。」

子曰：「吾未見剛者。」或對曰：「申根。」子曰：「根也慾，焉得剛？」

子貢曰：「我不欲人之加諸我也，吾亦欲無加諸人。」子曰：「賜也，非爾所及也。」

子谓子贡曰：「女与回也孰愈？」对曰：「赐也何敢望回。回也闻一以知十，赐也闻一以知二。」子曰：「弗如也！吾与女弗如也。」

宰予昼寝。子曰：「朽木不可雕也，粪土之墙不可杇也，于予与何诛。」子曰：「始吾于人也，听其言而信其行；今吾于人也，听其言而观其行。于予与改是。」

子曰：「吾未见刚者。」或对曰：「申枨。」子曰：「枨也欲，焉得刚？」

子贡曰：「我不欲人之加诸我也，吾亦欲无加诸人。」子曰：「赐也，非尔所及也。」

CHAP. VII. 1. The Master said to Tsze-kung, 'Which do you consider superior, yourself or Hui?' 2. Tsze-kung replied, 'How dare I compare myself with Hui? Hui hears one point and knows all about a subject; I hear one point, and know a second.' 3. The Master said, 'You are not equal to him. I grant you, you are not equal to him.'

CHAP. IX. 1. Tsai Yu being asleep during the daytime, the Master said, 'Rotten wood cannot be carved; a wall of dirty earth will not receive the trowel. This Yu!— what is the use of my reproving him?' 2. The Master said, 'At first, my way with men was to hear their words, and give them credit for their conduct. Now my way is to hear their words, and look at their conduct. It is from Yu that I have learned to make this change.'

CHAP. X. The Master said, 'I have not seen a firm and unbending man.' Some one replied, 'There is Shan Ch'ang.' 'Ch'ang,' said the Master, 'is under the influence of his passions; how can he be pronounced firm and unbending?'

CHAP. XI. Tsze-kung said, 'What I do not wish men to do to me, I also wish not to do to men.' The Master said, 'Ts'ze, you have not attained to that.'

SEAL SCRIPT

子貢曰：「夫子之文章，可得而聞也；夫子之言性與天道，不可得而聞也。」

子路有聞，未之能行，唯恐有聞。

子貢問曰：「孔文子何以謂之文也？」子曰：「敏而好學，不恥下問，是以謂之文也。」

子謂子產，「有君子之道四焉：其行己也恭，其事上也敬，其養民也惠，其使民也義。」

子曰：「晏平仲善與人交，久而敬之。」

子曰：「臧文仲居蔡，山節藻梲，何如其知也？」

子贡曰：「夫子之文章，可得而闻也；夫子之言性与天道，不可得而闻也。」

子路有闻，未之能行，唯恐有闻。

子贡问曰：「孔文子何以谓之文也？」子曰：「敏而好学，不耻下问，是以谓之文也。」

子谓子产，「有君子之道四焉：其行己也恭，其事上也敬，其养民也惠，其使民也义。」

子曰：「晏平仲善与人交，久而敬之。」

子曰：「臧文仲居蔡，山节藻梲，何如其知也？」

CHAP. XII. Tsze-kung said, 'The Master's personal displays of his principles and ordinary descriptions of them may be heard. His discourses about man's nature, and the way of Heaven, cannot be heard.'

CHAP. XIII. When Tsze-lu heard anything, if he had not yet succeeded in carrying it into practice, he was only afraid lest he should hear something else.

CHAP. XIV. Tsze-kung asked, saying, 'On what ground did Kung-wan get that title of Wan?' The Master said, 'He was of an active nature and yet fond of learning, and he was not ashamed to ask and learn of his inferiors!— On these grounds he has been styled Wan.'

CHAP. XV. The Master said of Tsze-ch'an that he had four of the characteristics of a superior man:— in his conduct of himself, he was humble; in serving his superiors, he was respectful; in nourishing the people, he was kind; in ordering the people, he was just.'

CHAP. XVI. The Master said, 'Yen P'ing knew well how to maintain friendly intercourse. The acquaintance might be long, but he showed the same respect as at first.'

CHAP. XVII. The Master said, 'Tsang Wan kept a large tortoise in a house, on the capitals of the pillars of which he had hills made, and with representations of duckweed on the small pillars above the beams supporting the rafters.— Of what sort was his wisdom?'

SEAL SCRIPT

　　子張問曰：「令尹子文三仕為令尹，無喜色；三已之，無慍色。舊令尹之政，必以告新令尹。何如？」子曰：「忠矣。」曰：「仁矣乎？」曰：「未知，焉得仁？」「崔子弒齊君，陳文子有馬十乘，棄而違之。至於他邦，則曰：『猶吾大夫崔子也。』違之。之一邦，則又曰：『猶吾大夫崔子也。』違之。何如？」子曰：「清矣。」曰：「仁矣乎？」曰：「未知。焉得仁？」

　　季文子三思而後行。子聞之，曰：「再，斯可矣。」

　　子曰：「甯武子邦有道則知，邦無道則愚。其知可及也，其愚不可及也。」

　　子张问曰：「令尹子文三仕为令尹，无喜色；三已之，无慍色。旧令尹之政，必以告新令尹。何如？」子曰：「忠矣。」曰：「仁矣乎？」曰：「未知，焉得仁？」「崔子弒齐君，陈文子有马十乘，弃而违之。至于他邦，则曰：『犹吾大夫崔子也。』违之。之一邦，则又曰：『犹吾大夫崔子也。』违之。何如？」子曰：「清矣。」曰：「仁矣乎？」曰：「未知。焉得仁？」

　　季文子三思而后行。子闻之，曰：「再，斯可矣。」

　　子曰：「宁武子邦有道则知，邦无道则愚。其知可及也，其愚不可及也。」

CHAP. XVIII. 1. Tsze-chang asked, saying, 'The minister Tsze- wan thrice took office, and manifested no joy in his countenance. Thrice he retired from office, and manifested no displeasure. He made it a point to inform the new minister of the way in which he had conducted the government;— what do you say of him?' The Master replied. 'He was loyal.' 'Was he perfectly virtuous?' 'I do not know. How can he be pronounced perfectly virtuous?' 2. Tsze-chang proceeded, 'When the officer Ch'ui killed the prince of Ch'i, Ch'an Wan, though he was the owner of forty horses, abandoned them and left the country. Coming to another State, he said, "They are here like our great officer, Ch'ui," and left it. He came to a second State, and with the same observation left it also;— what do you say of him?' The Master replied, 'He was pure.' 'Was he perfectly virtuous?' 'I do not know. How can he be pronounced perfectly virtuous?'

CHAP. XIX. Chi Wan thought thrice, and then acted. When the Master was informed of it, he said, 'Twice may do.'

CHAP. XX. The Master said, 'When good order prevailed in his country, Ning Wu acted the part of a wise man. When his country was in disorder, he acted the part of a stupid man. Others may equal his wisdom, but they cannot equal his stupidity.'

SEAL SCRIPT

　　子在陳曰：「歸與！歸與！吾黨之小子狂簡，斐然成章，不知所以裁之。」

　　子曰：「伯夷、叔齊不念舊惡，怨是用希。」

　　子曰：「孰謂微生高直？或乞醯焉，乞諸其鄰而與之。」

　　子曰：「巧言、令色、足恭，左丘明恥之，丘亦恥之。匿怨而友其人，左丘明恥之，丘亦恥之。」

　　子在陈曰：「归与！归与！吾党之小子狂简，斐然成章，不知所以裁之。」

　　子曰：「伯夷、叔齐不念旧恶，怨是用希。」

　　子曰：「孰谓微生高直？或乞醯焉，乞诸其邻而与之。」

　　子曰：「巧言、令色、足恭，左丘明耻之，丘亦耻之。匿怨而友其人，左丘明耻之，丘亦耻之。」

CHAP. XXI. When the Master was in Ch'an, he said, 'Let me return! Let me return! The little children of my school are ambitious and too hasty. They are accomplished and complete so far, but they do not know how to restrict and shape themselves.'

CHAP. XXII. The Master said, 'Po-i and Shu-ch'i did not keep the former wickednesses of men in mind, and hence the resentments directed towards them were few.'

CHAP. XXIII. The Master said, 'Who says of Wei-shang Kao that he is upright? One begged some vinegar of him, and he begged it of a neighbor and gave it to the man.'

CHAP. XXIV. The Master said, 'Fine words, an insinuating appearance, and excessive respect;— Tso Ch'iu-ming was ashamed of them. I also am ashamed of them. To conceal resentment against a person, and appear friendly with him;— Tso Ch'iu-ming was ashamed of such conduct. I also am ashamed of it.'

SEAL SCRIPT

顏淵、季路侍。子曰：「盍各言爾志？」子路曰：「願車馬、衣輕裘，與朋友共。敝之而無憾。」顏淵曰：「願無伐善，無施勞。」子路曰：「願聞子之志。」子曰：「老者安之，朋友信之，少者懷之。」

子曰：「已矣乎！吾未見能見其過而內自訟者也。」

子曰：「十室之邑，必有忠信如丘者焉，不如丘之好學也。」

颜渊、季路侍。子曰：「盍各言尔志？」子路曰：「愿车马、衣轻裘，与朋友共。敝之而无憾。」颜渊曰：「愿无伐善，无施劳。」子路曰：「愿闻子之志。」子曰：「老者安之，朋友信之，少者怀之。」

子曰：「已矣乎！吾未见能见其过而内自讼者也。」

子曰：「十室之邑，必有忠信如丘者焉，不如丘之好学也。」

CHAP. XXV. 1. Yen Yuan and Chi Lu being by his side, the Master said to them, 'Come, let each of you tell his wishes.' 2. Tsze-lu said, 'I should like, having chariots and horses, and light fur dresses, to share them with my friends, and though they should spoil them, I would not be displeased.' 3. Yen Yuan said, 'I should like not to boast of my excellence, nor to make a display of my meritorious deeds.' 4. Tsze-lu then said, 'I should like, sir, to hear your wishes.' The Master said, 'They are, in regard to the aged, to give them rest; in regard to friends, to show them sincerity; in regard to the young, to treat them tenderly.'

CHAP. XXVI. The Master said, 'It is all over! I have not yet seen one who could perceive his faults, and inwardly accuse himself.'

CHAP. XXVII. The Master said, 'In a hamlet of ten families, there may be found one honourable and sincere as I am, but not so fond of learning.'

SEAL SCRIPT

雍也第六

子曰：「雍也可使南面。」

仲弓問子桑伯子，子曰：「可也簡。」仲弓曰：「居敬而行簡，以臨其民，不亦可乎？居簡而行簡，無乃大簡乎？」子曰：「雍之言然。」

哀公問：「弟子孰為好學？」孔子對曰：「有顏回者好學，不遷怒，不貳過。不幸短命死矣！今也則亡，未聞好學者也。」

SIMPLIFIED CHINESE

雍也第六

子曰：「雍也可使南面。」

仲弓问子桑伯子，子曰：「可也简。」仲弓曰：「居敬而行简，以临其民，不亦可乎？居简而行简，无乃大简乎？」子曰：「雍之言然。」

哀公问：「弟子孰为好学？」孔子对曰：「有颜回者好学，不迁怒，不贰过。不幸短命死矣！今也则亡，未闻好学者也。」

BOOK VI. YUNG YEY.

CHAP. I. 1. The Master said, 'There is Yung!— He might occupy the place of a prince.' 2. Chung-kung asked about Tsze-sang Po-tsze. The Master said, 'He may pass. He does not mind small matters.' 3. Chung-kung said, 'If a man cherish in himself a reverential feeling of the necessity of attention to business, though he may be easy in small matters in his government of the people, that may be allowed. But if he cherish in himself that easy feeling, and also carry it out in his practice, is not such an easy mode of procedure excessive?' 4. The Master said, 'Yung's words are right.'

CHAP. II. The Duke Ai asked which of the disciples loved to learn. Confucius replied to him, 'There was Yen Hui; HE loved to learn. He did not transfer his anger; he did not repeat a fault. Unfortunately, his appointed time was short and he died; and now there is not such another. I have not yet heard of any one who loves to learn as he did.'

SEAL SCRIPT

　　子華使於齊，冉子為其母請粟。子曰：「與之釜。」請益。曰：「與之庾。」冉子與之粟五秉。子曰：「赤之適齊也，乘肥馬，衣輕裘。吾聞之也，君子周急不繼富。」

　　原思為之宰，與之粟九百，辭。子曰：「毋！以與爾鄉里鄉黨乎！」

　　子謂仲弓曰：「犁牛之子騂且角，雖欲勿用，山川其舍諸？」

　　子曰：「回也，其心三月不違仁，其餘則日月至焉而已矣。」

　　子华使于齐，冉子为其母请粟。子曰：「与之釜。」请益。曰：「与之庾。」冉子与之粟五秉。子曰：「赤之适齐也，乘肥马，衣轻裘。吾闻之也，君子周急不继富。」

　　原思为之宰，与之粟九百，辞。子曰：「毋！以与尔邻里乡党乎！」

　　子谓仲弓曰：「犁牛之子骍且角，虽欲勿用，山川其舍诸？」

　　子曰：「回也，其心三月不违仁，其余则日月至焉而已矣。」

CHAP. III. 1. Tsze-hwa being employed on a mission to Ch'i, the disciple Zan requested grain for his mother. The Master said, 'Give her a fu.' Yen requested more. 'Give her an yu,' said the Master. Yen gave her five ping. 2. The Master said, 'When Ch'ih was proceeding to Ch'i, he had fat horses to his carriage, and wore light furs. I have heard that a superior man helps the distressed, but does not add to the wealth of the rich.' 3. Yuan Sze being made governor of his town by the Master, he gave him nine hundred measures of grain, but Sze declined them. 4. The Master said, 'Do not decline them. May you not give them away in the neighborhoods, hamlets, towns, and villages?'

CHAP. IV. The Master, speaking of Chung-kung, said, 'If the calf of a brindled cow be red and horned, although men may not wish to use it, would the spirits of the mountains and rivers put it aside?'

CHAP. V. The Master said, 'Such was Hui that for three months there would be nothing in his mind contrary to perfect virtue. The others may attain to this on some days or in some months, but nothing more.'

SEAL SCRIPT

季康子問：「仲由可使從政也與？」子曰：「由也果，於從政乎何有？」曰：「賜也，可使從政也與？」曰：「賜也達，於從政乎何有？」曰：「求也，可使從政也與？」曰：「求也藝，於從政乎何有？」

季氏使閔子騫為費宰。閔子騫曰：「善為我辭焉。如有復我者，則吾必在汶上矣。」

伯牛有疾，子問之，自牖執其手，曰：「亡之，命矣夫！斯人也而有斯疾也！斯人也而有斯疾也！」

子曰：「賢哉回也！一簞食，一瓢飲，在陋巷。人不堪其憂，回也不改其樂。賢哉回也！」

季康子问：「仲由可使从政也与？」子曰：「由也果，于从政乎何有？」曰：「赐也，可使从政也与？」曰：「赐也达，于从政乎何有？」曰：「求也，可使从政也与？」曰：「求也艺，于从政乎何有？」

季氏使闵子骞为费宰。闵子骞曰：「善为我辞焉。如有复我者，则吾必在汶上矣。」

伯牛有疾，子问之，自牖执其手，曰：「亡之，命矣夫！斯人也而有斯疾也！斯人也而有斯疾也！」

子曰：「贤哉回也！一箪食，一瓢饮，在陋巷。人不堪其忧，回也不改其乐。贤哉回也！」

CHAP. VI. Chi K'ang asked about Chung-yu, whether he was fit to be employed as an officer of government. The Master said, 'Yu is a man of decision; what difficulty would he find in being an officer of government?' K'ang asked, 'Is Ts'ze fit to be employed as an officer of government?' and was answered, 'Ts'ze is a man of intelligence; what difficulty would he find in being an officer of government?' And to the same question about Ch'iu the Master gave the same reply, saying, 'Ch'iu is a man of various ability.'

CHAP. VII. The chief of the Chi family sent to ask Min Tsze-ch'ien to be governor of Pi. Min Tsze-ch'ien said, 'Decline the offer for me politely. If any one come again to me with a second invitation, I shall be obliged to go and live on the banks of the Wan.'

CHAP. VIII. Po-niu being ill, the Master went to ask for him. He took hold of his hand through the window, and said, 'It is killing him. It is the appointment of Heaven, alas! That such a man should have such a sickness! That such a man should have such a sickness!'

CHAP. IX. The Master said, 'Admirable indeed was the virtue of Hui! With a single bamboo dish of rice, a single gourd dish of drink, and living in his mean narrow lane, while others could not have endured the distress, he did not allow his joy to be affected by it. Admirable indeed was the virtue of Hui!'

SEAL SCRIPT

　　冉求曰：「非不說子之道，力不足也。」子曰：「力不足者，中道而廢。今女畫。」

　　子謂子夏曰：「女為君子儒，無為小人儒。」

　　子游為武城宰。子曰：「女得人焉爾乎？」曰：「有澹臺滅明者，行不由徑。非公事，未嘗至於偃之室也。」

　　子曰：「孟之反不伐，奔而殿。將入門，策其馬，曰：『非敢後也，馬不進也。』」

　　子曰：「不有祝鮀之佞而有宋朝之美，難乎免於今之世矣！」

　　子曰：「誰能出不由戶？何莫由斯道也？」

　　冉求曰：「非不说子之道，力不足也。」子曰：「力不足者，中道而废。今女画。」

　　子谓子夏曰：「女为君子儒，无为小人儒。」

　　子游为武城宰。子曰：「女得人焉尔乎？」曰：「有澹台灭明者，行不由径。非公事，未尝至于偃之室也。」

　　子曰：「孟之反不伐，奔而殿。将入门，策其马，曰：『非敢后也，马不进也。』」

　　子曰：「不有祝鮀之佞而有宋朝之美，难乎免于今之世矣！」

　　子曰：「谁能出不由户？何莫由斯道也？」

CHAP. X. Yen Ch'iu said, 'It is not that I do not delight in your doctrines, but my strength is insufficient.' The Master said, 'Those whose strength is insufficient give over in the middle of the way but now you limit yourself.'

CHAP. XI. The Master said to Tsze-hsia, 'Do you be a scholar after the style of the superior man, and not after that of the mean man.'

CHAP. XII. Tsze-yu being governor of Wu-ch'ang, the Master said to him, 'Have you got good men there?' He answered, 'There is Tan-t'ai Mieh-ming, who never in walking takes a short cut, and never comes to my office, excepting on public business.'

CHAP. XIII. The Master said, 'Mang Chih-fan does not boast of his merit. Being in the rear on an occasion of flight, when they were about to enter the gate, he whipped up his horse, saying, "It is not that I dare to be last. My horse would not advance."'

CHAP. XIV. The Master said, 'Without the specious speech of the litanist T'o and the beauty of the prince Chao of Sung, it is difficult to escape in the present age.'

CHAP. XV. The Master said, 'Who can go out but by the door? How is it that men will not walk according to these ways?'

SEAL SCRIPT

69

　　子曰：「質勝文則野，文勝質則史。文質彬彬，然後君子。」
　　子曰：「人之生也直，罔之生也幸而免。」
　　子曰：「知之者不如好之者，好之者不如樂之者。」
　　子曰：「中人以上，可以語上也；中人以下，不可以語上也。」
　　樊遲問知。子曰：「務民之義，敬鬼神而遠之，可謂知矣。」
問仁。曰：「仁者先難而後獲，可謂仁矣。」

　　子曰：「质胜文则野，文胜质则史。文质彬彬，然后君子。」
　　子曰：「人之生也直，罔之生也幸而免。」
　　子曰：「知之者不如好之者，好之者不如乐之者。」
　　子曰：「中人以上，可以语上也；中人以下，不可以语上也。」
　　樊迟问知。子曰：「务民之义，敬鬼神而远之，可谓知矣。」
问仁。曰：「仁者先难而后获，可谓仁矣。」

CHAP. XVI. The Master said, 'Where the solid qualities are in excess of accomplishments, we have rusticity; where the accomplishments are in excess of the solid qualities, we have the manners of a clerk. When the accomplishments and solid qualities are equally blended, we then have the man of virtue.'

CHAP. XVII. The Master said, 'Man is born for uprightness. If a man lose his uprightness, and yet live, his escape from death is the effect of mere good fortune.'

CHAP. XVIII. The Master said, 'They who know the truth are not equal to those who love it, and they who love it are not equal to those who delight in it.'

CHAP. XIX. The Master said, 'To those whose talents are above mediocrity, the highest subjects may be announced. To those who are below mediocrity, the highest subjects may not be announced.'

CHAP. XX. Fan Ch'ih asked what constituted wisdom. The Master said, 'To give one's self earnestly to the duties due to men, and, while respecting spiritual beings, to keep aloof from them, may be called wisdom.' He asked about perfect virtue. The Master said, 'The man of virtue makes the difficulty to be overcome his first business, and success only a subsequent consideration;— this may be called perfect virtue.'

SEAL SCRIPT

子曰：「知者樂水，仁者樂山；知者動，仁者靜；知者樂，仁者壽。」

子曰：「齊一變，至於魯；魯一變，至於道。」

子曰：「觚不觚，觚哉！觚哉！」

宰我問曰：「仁者，雖告之曰：『井有仁焉。』其從之也？」子曰：「何為其然也？君子可逝也，不可陷也；可欺也，不可罔也。」

子曰：「君子博學於文，約之以禮，亦可以弗畔矣夫！」

子見南子，子路不說。夫子矢之曰：「予所否者，天厭之！天厭之！」

子曰：「知者乐水，仁者乐山；知者动，仁者静；知者乐，仁者寿。」

子曰：「齐一变，至于鲁；鲁一变，至于道。」

子曰：「觚不觚，觚哉！觚哉！」

宰我问曰：「仁者，虽告之曰：『井有仁焉。』其从之也？」子曰：「何为其然也？君子可逝也，不可陷也；可欺也，不可罔也。」

子曰：「君子博学于文，约之以礼，亦可以弗畔矣夫！」

子见南子，子路不说。夫子矢之曰：「予所否者，天厌之！天厌之！」

CHAP. XXI. The Master said, 'The wise find pleasure in water; the virtuous find pleasure in hills. The wise are active; the virtuous are tranquil. The wise are joyful; the virtuous are long-lived.'

CHAP. XXII. The Master said, 'Ch'i, by one change, would come to the State of Lu. Lu, by one change, would come to a State where true principles predominated.'

CHAP. XXIII. The Master said, 'A cornered vessel without corners.— A strange cornered vessel! A strange cornered vessel!'

CHAP. XXIV. Tsai Wo asked, saying, 'A benevolent man, though it be told him,— 'There is a man in the well' will go in after him, I suppose.' Confucius said, 'Why should he do so?' A superior man may be made to go to the well, but he cannot be made to go down into it. He may be imposed upon, but he cannot be fooled.'

CHAP. XXV. The Master said, 'The superior man, extensively studying all learning, and keeping himself under the restraint of the rules of propriety, may thus likewise not overstep what is right.'

CHAP. XXVI. The Master having visited Nan-tsze, Tsze-lu was displeased, on which the Master swore, saying, 'Wherein I have done improperly, may Heaven reject me, may Heaven reject me!'

SEAL SCRIPT

　　子曰：「中庸之為德也，其至矣乎！民鮮久矣。」
　　子貢曰：「如有博施於民而能濟眾，何如？可謂仁乎？」子曰：「何事於仁，必也聖乎！堯舜其猶病諸！夫仁者，己欲立而立人，己欲達而達人。能近取譬，可謂仁之方也已。」

　　子曰：「中庸之为德也，其至矣乎！民鲜久矣。」
　　子贡曰：「如有博施于民而能济众，何如？可谓仁乎？」子曰：「何事于仁，必也圣乎！尧舜其犹病诸！夫仁者，己欲立而立人，己欲达而达人。能近取譬，可谓仁之方也已。」

CHAP. XXVII. The Master said, 'Perfect is the virtue which is according to the Constant Mean! Rare for a long time has been its practise among the people.'

CHAP. XXVIII. 1. Tsze-kung said, 'Suppose the case of a man extensively conferring benefits on the people, and able to assist all, what would you say of him? Might he be called perfectly virtuous?' The Master said, 'Why speak only of virtue in connexion with him? Must he not have the qualities of a sage? Even Yao and Shun were still solicitous about this. 2. 'Now the man of perfect virtue, wishing to be established himself, seeks also to establish others; wishing to be enlarged himself, he seeks also to enlarge others. 3. 'To be able to judge of others by what is nigh in ourselves;— this may be called the art of virtue.'

SEAL SCRIPT

述而第七

子曰：「述而不作，信而好古，竊比於我老彭。」

子曰：「默而識之，學而不厭，誨人不倦，何有於我哉？」

子曰：「德之不脩，學之不講，聞義不能徙，不善不能改，是吾憂也。」

子之燕居，申申如也，夭夭如也。

子曰：「甚矣吾衰也！久矣吾不復夢見周公。」

子曰：「志於道，據於德，依於仁，游於藝。」

述而第七

子曰：「述而不作，信而好古，窃比于我老彭。」

子曰：「默而识之，学而不厌，诲人不倦，何有于我哉？」

子曰：「德之不修，学之不讲，闻义不能徙，不善不能改，是吾忧也。」

子之燕居，申申如也，夭夭如也。

子曰：「甚矣吾衰也！久矣吾不复梦见周公。」

子曰：「志于道，据于德，依于仁，游于艺。」

BOOK VII. SHU R.

CHAP. I. The Master said, 'A transmitter and not a maker, believing in and loving the ancients, I venture to compare myself with our old P'ang.'

CHAP. II. The Master said, 'The silent treasuring up of knowledge; learning without satiety; and instructing others without being wearied:— which one of these things belongs to me?'

CHAP. III. The Master said, 'The leaving virtue without proper cultivation; the not thoroughly discussing what is learned; not being able to move towards righteousness of which a knowledge is gained; and not being able to change what is not good:— these are the things which occasion me solicitude.'

CHAP. IV. When the Master was unoccupied with business, his manner was easy, and he looked pleased.

CHAP. V. The Master said, 'Extreme is my decay. For a long time, I have not dreamed, as I was wont to do, that I saw the duke of Chau.'

CHAP. VI. 1. The Master said, 'Let the will be set on the path of duty. 2. 'Let every attainment in what is good be firmly grasped. 3. 'Let perfect virtue be accorded with. 4. 'Let relaxation and enjoyment be found in the polite arts.'

SEAL SCRIPT

子曰：「自行束脩以上，吾未嘗無誨焉。」

子曰：「不憤不啟，不悱不發，舉一隅不以三隅反，則不復也。」

子食於有喪者之側，未嘗飽也。

子於是日哭，則不歌。

子謂顏淵曰：「用之則行，舍之則藏，唯我與爾有是夫！」子路曰：「子行三軍，則誰與？」子曰：「暴虎馮河，死而無悔者，吾不與也。必也臨事而懼，好謀而成者也。」

子曰：「富而可求也，雖執鞭之士，吾亦為之。如不可求，從吾所好。」

子曰：「自行束修以上，吾未尝无诲焉。」

子曰：「不愤不启，不悱不发，举一隅不以三隅反，则不复也。」

子食于有丧者之侧，未尝饱也。

子于是日哭，则不歌。

子谓颜渊曰：「用之则行，舍之则藏，唯我与尔有是夫！」子路曰：「子行三军，则谁与？」子曰：「暴虎冯河，死而无悔者，吾不与也。必也临事而惧，好谋而成者也。」

子曰：「富而可求也，虽执鞭之士，吾亦为之。如不可求，从吾所好。」

CHAP. VII. The Master said, 'From the man bringing his bundle of dried flesh for my teaching upwards, I have never refused instruction to any one.'

CHAP. VIII. The Master said, 'I do not open up the truth to one who is not eager to get knowledge, nor help out any one who is not anxious to explain himself. When I have presented one corner of a subject to any one, and he cannot from it learn the other three, I do not repeat my lesson.'

CHAP. IX. 1. When the Master was eating by the side of a mourner, he never ate to the full. 2. He did not sing on the same day in which he had been weeping.

CHAP. X. 1. The Master said to Yen Yuan, 'When called to office, to under-take its duties; when not so called, to lie retired;— it is only I and you who have attained to this.' 2. Tsze-lu said, 'If you had the conduct of the armies of a great State, whom would you have to act with you?' 3. The Master said, 'I would not have him to act with me, who will unarmed attack a tiger, or cross a river without a boat, dying without any regret. My associate must be the man who proceeds to action full of solicitude, who is fond of adjusting his plans, and then carries them into execution.'

CHAP. XI. The Master said, 'If the search for riches is sure to be successful, though I should become a groom with whip in hand to get them, I will do so. As the search may not be successful, I will follow after that which I love.'

SEAL SCRIPT

子之所慎：齊，戰，疾。

子在齊聞韶，三月不知肉味。曰：「不圖為樂之至於斯也！」

冉有曰：「夫子為衛君乎？」子貢曰：「諾。吾將問之。」入，曰：「伯夷、叔齊何人也？」曰：「古之賢人也。」曰：「怨乎？」曰：「求仁而得仁，又何怨。」出，曰：「夫子不為也。」

子曰：「飯疏食飲水，曲肱而枕之，樂亦在其中矣。不義而富且貴，於我如浮雲。」

子曰：「加我數年，五十以學易，可以無大過矣。」

子之所慎：齐，战，疾。

子在齐闻韶，三月不知肉味。曰：「不图为乐之至于斯也！」

冉有曰：「夫子为卫君乎？」子贡曰：「诺。吾将问之。」入，曰：「伯夷、叔齐何人也？」曰：「古之贤人也。」曰：「怨乎？」曰：「求仁而得仁，又何怨。」出，曰：「夫子不为也。」

子曰：「饭疏食饮水，曲肱而枕之，乐亦在其中矣。不义而富且贵，于我如浮云。」

子曰：「加我数年，五十以学易，可以无大过矣。」

CHAP. XII. The things in reference to which the Master exercised the greatest caution were — fasting, war, and sickness.

CHAP. XIII. When the Master was in Ch'i, he heard the Shao, and for three months did not know the taste of flesh. 'I did not think" he said, 'that music could have been made so excellent as this.'

CHAP. XIV. 1. Yen Yu said, 'Is our Master for the ruler of Wei?' Tsze-kung said, 'Oh! I will ask him.' 2. He went in accordingly, and said, 'What sort of men were Po-i and Shu-ch'i?' 'They were ancient worthies,' said the Master. 'Did they have any repinings because of their course?' The Master again replied, 'They sought to act virtuously, and they did so; what was there for them to repine about?' On this, Tsze-kung went out and said, 'Our Master is not for him.'

CHAP. XV. The Master said, 'With coarse rice to eat, with water to drink, and my bended arm for a pillow;— I have still joy in the midst of these things. Riches and honours acquired by unrighteousness, are to me as a floating cloud.'

CHAP. XVI. The Master said, 'If some years were added to my life, I would give fifty to the study of the Yi, and then I might come to be without great faults.'

SEAL SCRIPT

81

子所雅言，詩、書、執禮，皆雅言也。

葉公問孔子於子路，子路不對。子曰：「女奚不曰，其為人也，發憤忘食，樂以忘憂，不知老之將至云爾。」

子曰：「我非生而知之者，好古，敏以求之者也。」

子不語怪，力，亂，神。

子曰：「三人行，必有我師焉。擇其善者而從之，其不善者而改之。」

子曰：「天生德於予，桓魋其如予何？」

子曰：「二三子以我為隱乎？吾無隱乎爾。吾無行而不與二三子者，是丘也。」

子所雅言，诗、书、执礼，皆雅言也。

叶公问孔子于子路，子路不对。子曰：「女奚不曰，其为人也，发愤忘食，乐以忘忧，不知老之将至云尔。」

子曰：「我非生而知之者，好古，敏以求之者也。」

子不语怪，力，乱，神。

子曰：「三人行，必有我师焉。择其善者而从之，其不善者而改之。」

子曰：「天生德于予，桓魋其如予何？」

子曰：「二三子以我为隐乎？吾无隐乎尔。吾无行而不与二三子者，是丘也。」

CHAP. XVII The Master's frequent themes of discourse were— the Odes, the History, and the maintenance of the Rules of Propriety. On all these he frequently discoursed.

CHAP. XVIII. 1. The Duke of Sheh asked Tsze-lu about Confucius, and Tsze-lu did not answer him. 2. The Master said, 'Why did you not say to him,— He is simply a man, who in his eager pursuit (of knowledge) forgets his food, who in the joy of its attainment forgets his sorrows, and who does not perceive that old age is coming on?'

CHAP. XIX. The Master said, 'I am not one who was born in the possession of knowledge; I am one who is fond of antiquity, and earnest in seeking it there.'

CHAP. XX. The subjects on which the Master did not talk, were— extraordinary things, feats of strength, disorder, and spiritual beings.

CHAP. XXI. The Master said, 'When I walk along with two others, they may serve me as my teachers. I will select their good qualities and follow them, their bad qualities and avoid them.'

CHAP. XXII. The Master said, 'Heaven produced the virtue that is in me. Hwan T'ui— what can he do to me?'

CHAP. XXIII. The Master said, 'Do you think, my disciples, that I have any concealments? I conceal nothing from you. There is nothing which I do that is not shown to you, my disciples;— that is my way.'

SEAL SCRIPT

83

子以四教：文，行，忠，信。

子曰：「聖人，吾不得而見之矣；得見君子者，斯可矣。」子曰：「善人，吾不得而見之矣；得見有恆者，斯可矣。亡而為有，虛而為盈，約而為泰，難乎有恆矣。」

子釣而不綱，弋不射宿。

子曰：「蓋有不知而作之者，我無是也。多聞擇其善者而從之，多見而識之，知之次也。」

互鄉難與言，童子見，門人惑。子曰：「與其進也，不與其退也，唯何甚！人潔己以進，與其潔也，不保其往也。」

子以四教：文，行，忠，信。

子曰：「圣人，吾不得而见之矣；得见君子者，斯可矣。」子曰：「善人，吾不得而见之矣；得见有恒者，斯可矣。亡而为有，虚而为盈，约而为泰，难乎有恒矣。」

子钓而不纲，弋不射宿。

子曰：「盖有不知而作之者，我无是也。多闻择其善者而从之，多见而识之，知之次也。」

互乡难与言，童子见，门人惑。子曰：「与其进也，不与其退也，唯何甚！人洁己以进，与其洁也，不保其往也。」

CHAP. XXIV. There were four things which the Master taught,— letters, ethics, devotion of soul, and truthfulness.

CHAP. XXV. 1. The Master said, 'A sage it is not mine to see; could I see a man of real talent and virtue, that would satisfy me.' 2. The Master said, 'A good man it is not mine to see; could I see a man possessed of constancy, that would satisfy me. 3. 'Having not and yet affecting to have, empty and yet affecting to be full, straitened and yet affecting to be at ease:— it is difficult with such characteristics to have constancy.'

CHAP. XXVI. The Master angled,— but did not use a net. He shot,— but not at birds perching.

CHAP. XXVII. The Master said, 'There may be those who act without knowing why. I do not do so. Hearing much and selecting what is good and following it; seeing much and keeping it in memory:— this is the second style of knowledge.'

CHAP. XXVIII. 1. It was difficult to talk (profitably and reputably) with the people of Hu-hsiang, and a lad of that place having had an interview with the Master, the disciples doubted. 2. The Master said, 'I admit people's approach to me without committing myself as to what they may do when they have retired. Why must one be so severe? If a man purify himself to wait upon me, I receive him so purified, without guaranteeing his past conduct.'

SEAL SCRIPT

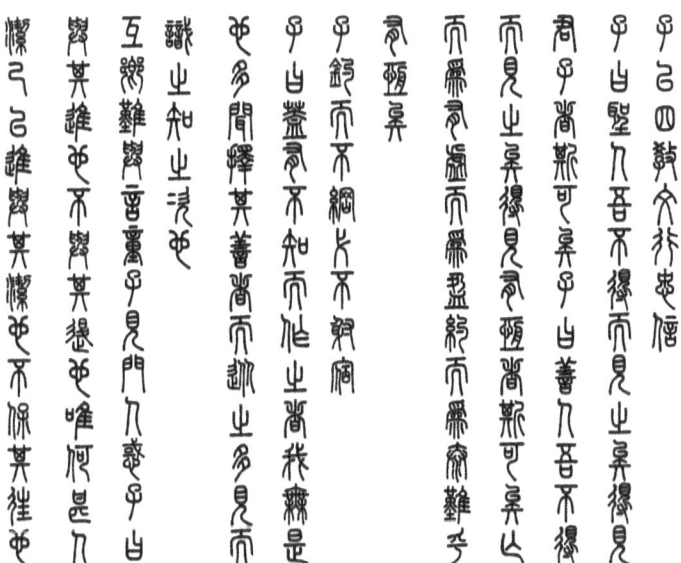

子曰：「仁遠乎哉？我欲仁，斯仁至矣。」

陳司敗問昭公知禮乎？孔子曰：「知禮。」孔子退，揖巫馬期而進之，曰：「吾聞君子不黨，君子亦黨乎？君取於吳為同姓，謂之吳孟子。君而知禮，孰不知禮？」巫馬期以告。子曰：「丘也幸，苟有過，人必知之。」

子與人歌而善，必使反之，而後和之。

子曰：「文，莫吾猶人也。躬行君子，則吾未之有得。」

子曰：「仁远乎哉？我欲仁，斯仁至矣。」

陈司败问昭公知礼乎？孔子曰：「知礼。」孔子退，揖巫马期而进之，曰：「吾闻君子不党，君子亦党乎？君取于吴为同姓，谓之吴孟子。君而知礼，孰不知礼？」巫马期以告。子曰：「丘也幸，苟有过，人必知之。」

子与人歌而善，必使反之，而后和之。

子曰：「文，莫吾犹人也。躬行君子，则吾未之有得。」

CHAP. XXIX. The Master said, 'Is virtue a thing remote? I wish to be virtuous, and lo! virtue is at hand.'

CHAP. XXX. 1. The minister of crime of Ch'an asked whether the duke Chao knew propriety, and Confucius said, 'He knew propriety.' 2. Confucius having retired, the minister bowed to Wu-ma Ch'i to come forward, and said, 'I have heard that the superior man is not a partisan. May the superior man be a partisan also? The prince married a daughter of the house of Wu, of the same surname with himself, and called her,— "The elder Tsze of Wu." If the prince knew propriety, who does not know it?' 3. Wu-ma Ch'i reported these remarks, and the Master said, 'I am fortunate! If I have any errors, people are sure to know them.'

CHAP. XXXI. When the Master was in company with a person who was singing, if he sang well, he would make him repeat the song, while he accompanied it with his own voice.

CHAP. XXXII. The Master said, 'In letters I am perhaps equal to other men, but the character of the superior man, carrying out in his conduct what he professes, is what I have not yet attained to.'

SEAL SCRIPT

子曰仁遠乎哉我欲仁斯仁至矣

陳司敗問昭公知禮乎孔子曰知禮孔子退揖巫馬期而進之曰吾聞君子不黨君子亦黨乎君取於吳為同姓謂之吳孟子君而知禮孰不知禮巫馬期以告子曰丘也幸苟有過人必知之

子與人歌而善必使反之而後和之

子曰文莫吾猶人也躬行君子則吾未之有得

子曰：「若聖與仁，則吾豈敢？抑為之不厭，誨人不倦，則可謂云爾已矣。」公西華曰：「正唯弟子不能學也。」

子疾病，子路請禱。子曰：「有諸？」子路對曰：「有之。誄曰：『禱爾于上下神祇。』」子曰：「丘之禱久矣。」

子曰：「奢則不孫，儉則固。與其不孫也，寧固。」

子曰：「君子坦蕩蕩，小人長戚戚。」

子溫而厲，威而不猛，恭而安。

子曰：「若圣与仁，则吾岂敢？抑为之不厌，诲人不倦，则可谓云尔已矣。」公西华曰：「正唯弟子不能学也。」

子疾病，子路请祷。子曰：「有诸？」子路对曰：「有之。诔曰：『祷尔于上下神祇。』」子曰：「丘之祷久矣。」

子曰：「奢则不孙，俭则固。与其不孙也，宁固。」

子曰：「君子坦荡荡，小人长戚戚。」

子温而厉，威而不猛，恭而安。

CHAP. XXXIII. The Master said, 'The sage and the man of perfect virtue;— how dare I rank myself with them? It may simply be said of me, that I strive to become such without satiety, and teach others without weariness.' Kung-hsi Hwa said, 'This is just what we, the disciples, cannot imitate you in.'

CHAP. XXXIV. The Master being very sick, Tsze-lu asked leave to pray for him. He said, 'May such a thing be done?' Tsze-lu replied, 'It may. In the Eulogies it is said, "Prayer has been made for thee to the spirits of the upper and lower worlds."' The Master said, 'My praying has been for a long time.'

CHAP. XXXV. The Master said, 'Extravagance leads to insubordination, and parsimony to meanness. It is better to be mean than to be insubordinate.'

CHAP. XXXVI. The Master said, 'The superior man is satisfied and composed; the mean man is always full of distress.'

CHAP. XXXVII. The Master was mild, and yet dignified; majestic, and yet not fierce; respectful, and yet easy.

SEAL SCRIPT

泰伯第八

子曰：「泰伯，其可謂至德也已矣！三以天下讓，民無得而稱焉。」

子曰：「恭而無禮則勞，慎而無禮則葸，勇而無禮則亂，直而無禮則絞。君子篤於親，則民興於仁；故舊不遺，則民不偷。」

曾子有疾，召門弟子曰：「啟予足！啟予手！《詩》云『戰戰兢兢，如臨深淵，如履薄冰。』而今而後，吾知免夫！小子！」

泰伯第八

子曰：「泰伯，其可谓至德也已矣！三以天下让，民无得而称焉。」

子曰：「恭而无礼则劳，慎而无礼则葸，勇而无礼则乱，直而无礼则绞。君子笃于亲，则民兴于仁；故旧不遗，则民不偷。」

曾子有疾，召门弟子曰：「启予足！启予手！《诗》云『战战兢兢，如临深渊，如履薄冰。』而今而后，吾知免夫！小子！」

BOOK VIII. T'AI-PO.

CHAP. I. The Master said, 'T'ai-po may be said to have reached the highest point of virtuous action. Thrice he declined the kingdom, and the people in ignorance of his motives could not express their approbation of his conduct.'

CHAP. II. 1. The Master said, 'Respectfulness, without the rules of propriety, becomes laborious bustle; carefulness, without the rules of propriety, becomes timidity; boldness, without the rules of propriety, becomes insubordination; straightforwardness, without the rules of propriety, becomes rudeness. 2. 'When those who are in high stations perform well all their duties to their relations, the people are aroused to virtue. When old friends are not neglected by them, the people are preserved from meanness.'

CHAP. III. The philosopher Tsang being ill, he called to him the disciples of his school, and said, 'Uncover my feet, uncover my hands. It is said in the Book of Poetry, "We should be apprehensive and cautious, as if on the brink of a deep gulf, as if treading on thin ice," and so have I been. Now and hereafter, I know my escape from all injury to my person, O ye, my little children.'

SEAL SCRIPT

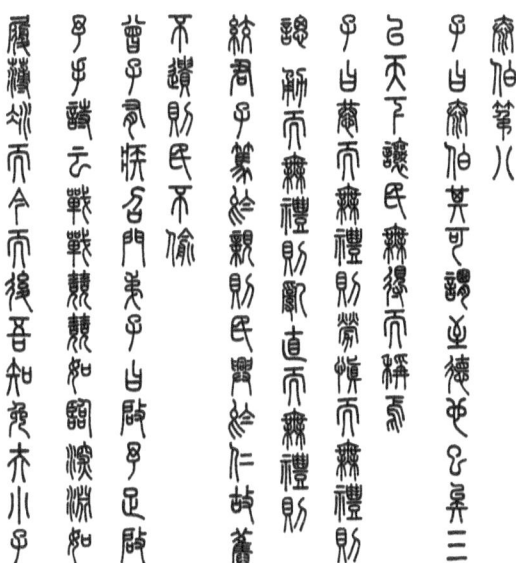

　　曾子有疾，孟敬子問之。曾子言曰：「鳥之將死，其鳴也哀；人之將死，其言也善。君子所貴乎道者三：動容貌，斯遠暴慢矣；正顏色，斯近信矣；出辭氣，斯遠鄙倍矣。籩豆之事，則有司存。」

　　曾子曰：「以能問於不能，以多問於寡；有若無，實若虛，犯而不校，昔者吾友嘗從事於斯矣。」

　　曾子曰：「可以託六尺之孤，可以寄百里之命，臨大節而不可奪也。君子人與？君子人也。」

　　曾子有疾，孟敬子问之。曾子言曰：「鸟之将死，其鸣也哀；人之将死，其言也善。君子所贵乎道者三：动容貌，斯远暴慢矣；正颜色，斯近信矣；出辞气，斯远鄙倍矣。笾豆之事，则有司存。」

　　曾子曰：「以能问于不能，以多问于寡；有若无，实若虚，犯而不校，昔者吾友尝从事于斯矣。」

　　曾子曰：「可以托六尺之孤，可以寄百里之命，临大节而不可夺也。君子人与？君子人也。」

CHAP. IV. 1. The philosopher Tsang being ill, Meng Chang went to ask how he was. 2. Tsang said to him, 'When a bird is about to die, its notes are mournful; when a man is about to die, his words are good. 3. 'There are three principles of conduct which the man of high rank should consider specially important:— that in his deportment and manner he keep from violence and heedlessness; that in regulating his countenance he keep near to sincerity; and that in his words and tones he keep far from lowness and impropriety. As to such matters as attending to the sacrificial vessels, there are the proper officers for them.'

CHAP. V. The philosopher Tsang said, 'Gifted with ability, and yet putting questions to those who were not so; possessed of much, and yet putting questions to those possessed of little; having, as though he had not; full, and yet counting himself as empty; offended against, and yet entering into no altercation; formerly I had a friend who pursued this style of conduct.'

CHAP. VI. The philosopher Tsang said, 'Suppose that there is an individual who can be entrusted with the charge of a young orphan prince, and can be commissioned with authority over a state of a hundred li, and whom no emergency however great can drive from his principles:— is such a man a superior man? He is a superior man indeed.'

SEAL SCRIPT

　　曾子曰：「士不可以不弘毅，任重而道遠。仁以為己任，不亦重乎？死而後已，不亦遠乎？」

　　子曰：「興於詩，立於禮。成於樂。」

　　子曰：「民可使由之，不可使知之。」

　　子曰：「好勇疾貧，亂也。人而不仁，疾之已甚，亂也。」

　　子曰：「如有周公之才之美，使驕且吝，其餘不足觀也已。」

　　子曰：「三年學，不至於穀，不易得也。」

　　曾子曰：「士不可以不弘毅，任重而道远。仁以为己任，不亦重乎？死而后已，不亦远乎？」

　　子曰：「兴于诗，立于礼。成于乐。」

　　子曰：「民可使由之，不可使知之。」

　　子曰：「好勇疾贫，乱也。人而不仁，疾之已甚，乱也。」

　　子曰：「如有周公之才之美，使骄且吝，其余不足观也已。」

　　子曰：「三年学，不至于谷，不易得也。」

CHAP. VII. 1. The philosopher Tsang said, 'The officer may not be without breadth of mind and vigorous endurance. His burden is heavy and his course is long. 2. 'Perfect virtue is the burden which he considers it is his to sustain;— is it not heavy? Only with death does his course stop;— is it not long?

CHAP. VIII. 1. The Master said, 'It is by the Odes that the mind is aroused. 2. 'It is by the Rules of Propriety that the character is established. 3. 'It is from Music that the finish is received.'

CHAP. IX. The Master said, 'The people may be made to follow a path of action, but they may not be made to understand it.'

CHAP. X. The Master said, 'The man who is fond of daring and is dissatisfied with poverty, will proceed to insubordination. So will the man who is not virtuous, when you carry your dislike of him to an extreme.'

CHAP. XI. The Master said, 'Though a man have abilities as admirable as those of the Duke of Chau, yet if he be proud and niggardly, those other things are really not worth being looked at.'

CHAP. XII. The Master said, 'It is not easy to find a man who has learned for three years without coming to be good.'

SEAL SCRIPT

子曰：「篤信好學，守死善道。危邦不入，亂邦不居。天下有道則見，無道則隱。邦有道，貧且賤焉，恥也；邦無道，富且貴焉，恥也。」

子曰：「不在其位，不謀其政。」

子曰：「師摯之始，關雎之亂，洋洋乎！盈耳哉。」

子曰：「狂而不直，侗而不愿，悾悾而不信，吾不知之矣。」

子曰：「學如不及，猶恐失之。」

子曰：「巍巍乎！舜禹之有天下也，而不與焉。」

子曰：「笃信好学，守死善道。危邦不入，乱邦不居。天下有道则见，无道则隐。邦有道，贫且贱焉，耻也；邦无道，富且贵焉，耻也。」

子曰：「不在其位，不谋其政。」

子曰：「师挚之始，关雎之乱，洋洋乎！盈耳哉。」

子曰：「狂而不直，侗而不愿，悾悾而不信，吾不知之矣。」

子曰：「学如不及，犹恐失之。」

子曰：「巍巍乎！舜禹之有天下也，而不与焉。」

CHAP. XIII. 1. The Master said, 'With sincere faith he unites the love of learning; holding firm to death, he is perfecting the excellence of his course. 2. 'Such an one will not enter a tottering State, nor dwell in a disorganized one. When right principles of government prevail in the kingdom, he will show himself; when they are prostrated, he will keep concealed. 3. 'When a country is well-governed, poverty and a mean condition are things to be ashamed of. When a country is ill- governed, riches and honour are things to be ashamed of.'

CHAP. XIV. The Master said, 'He who is not in any particular office, has nothing to do with plans for the administration of its duties.'

CHAP. XV. The Master said, 'When the music master Chih first entered on his office, the finish of the Kwan Tsu was magnificent;— how it filled the ears!'

CHAP. XVI. The Master said, 'Ardent and yet not upright; stupid and yet not attentive; simple and yet not sincere:— such persons I do not understand.'

CHAP. XVII. The Master said, 'Learn as if you could not reach your object, and were always fearing also lest you should lose it.'

CHAP. XVIII. The Master said, 'How majestic was the manner in which Shun and Yu held possession of the empire, as if it were nothing to them!'

SEAL SCRIPT

97

子曰：「大哉，堯之為君也！巍巍乎！唯天為大，唯堯則之。蕩蕩乎！民無能名焉。巍巍乎！其有成功也；煥乎，其有文章！」

舜有臣五人而天下治。武王曰：「予有亂臣十人。」孔子曰：「才難，不其然乎？唐虞之際，於斯為盛。有婦人焉，九人而已。三分天下有其二，以服事殷。周之德，其可謂至德也已矣。」

子曰：「禹，吾無間然矣。菲飲食，而致孝乎鬼神；惡衣服，而致美乎黻冕；卑宮室，而盡力乎溝洫。禹，吾無間然矣。」

子曰：「大哉，尧之为君也！巍巍乎！唯天为大，唯尧则之。荡荡乎！民无能名焉。巍巍乎！其有成功也；焕乎，其有文章！」

舜有臣五人而天下治。武王曰：「予有乱臣十人。」孔子曰：「才难，不其然乎？唐虞之际，于斯为盛。有妇人焉，九人而已。三分天下有其二，以服事殷。周之德，其可谓至德也已矣。」

子曰：「禹，吾无间然矣。菲饮食，而致孝乎鬼神；恶衣服，而致美乎黻冕；卑宫室，而尽力乎沟洫。禹，吾无间然矣。」

CHAP. XIX. 1. The Master said, 'Great indeed was Yao as a sovereign! How majestic was he! It is only Heaven that is grand, and only Yao corresponded to it. How vast was his virtue! The people could find no name for it. 2. 'How majestic was he in the works which he accomplished! How glorious in the elegant regulations which he instituted!'

CHAP. XX. 1. Shun had five ministers, and the empire was well-governed. 2. King Wu said, 'I have ten able ministers.' 3. Confucius said, 'Is not the saying that talents are difficult to find, true? Only when the dynasties of T'ang and Yu met, were they more abundant than in this of Chau, yet there was a woman among them. The able ministers were no more than nine men. 4. 'King Wan possessed two of the three parts of the empire, and with those he served the dynasty of Yin. The virtue of the house of Chau may be said to have reached the highest point indeed.'

CHAP. XXI. The Master said, 'I can find no flaw in the character of Yu. He used himself coarse food and drink, but displayed the utmost filial piety towards the spirits. His ordinary garments were poor, but he displayed the utmost elegance in his sacrificial cap and apron. He lived in a low mean house, but expended all his strength on the ditches and water-channels. I can find nothing like a flaw in Yu.'

SEAL SCRIPT

99

子罕第九

子罕言利，與命，與仁。

達巷黨人曰：「大哉孔子！博學而無所成名。」子聞之，謂門弟子曰：「吾何執？執御乎？執射乎？吾執御矣。」

子曰：「麻冕，禮也；今也純，儉。吾從眾。拜下，禮也；今拜乎上，泰也。雖違眾，吾從下。」

子絕四：*毋意，毋必，毋固，毋我*。

SIMPLIFIED CHINESE

子罕第九

子罕言利，与命，与仁。

达巷党人曰：「大哉孔子！博学而无所成名。」子闻之，谓门弟子曰：「吾何执？执御乎？执射乎？吾执御矣。」

子曰：「麻冕，礼也；今也纯，俭。吾从众。拜下，礼也；今拜乎上，泰也。虽违众，吾从下。」

子绝四：*毋意，毋必，毋固，毋我*。

BOOK IX. TSZE HAN.

CHAP. I. The subjects of which the Master seldom spoke were— profitableness, and also the appointments of Heaven, and perfect virtue.

CHAP. II. 1. A man of the village of Ta-hsiang said, 'Great indeed is the philosopher K'ung! His learning is extensive, and yet he does not render his name famous by any particular thing.' 2. The Master heard the observation, and said to his disciples, 'What shall I practise? Shall I practise charioteering, or shall I practise archery? I will practise charioteering.'

CHAP. III. 1. The Master said, 'The linen cap is that prescribed by the rules of ceremony, but now a silk one is worn. It is economical, and I follow the common practice. 2. 'The rules of ceremony prescribe the bowing below the hall, but now the practice is to bow only after ascending it. That is arrogant. I continue to bow below the hall, though I oppose the common practice.'

CHAP. IV. There were four things from which the Master was entirely free. He had no foregone conclusions, no arbitrary predeterminations, no obstinacy, and no egoism.

SEAL SCRIPT

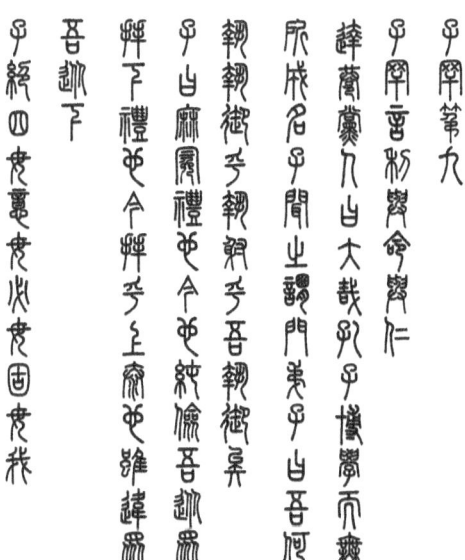

子畏於匡。曰：「文王既沒，文不在茲乎？天之將喪斯文也，後死者不得與於斯文也；天之未喪斯文也，匡人其如予何？」

大宰問於子貢曰：「夫子聖者與？何其多能也？」子貢曰：「固天縱之將聖，又多能也。」子聞之，曰：「大宰知我乎！吾少也賤，故多能鄙事。君子多乎哉？不多也。」

牢曰：「子云，『吾不試，故藝』。」

子曰：「吾有知乎哉？無知也。有鄙夫問於我，空空如也，我叩其兩端而竭焉。」

子曰：「鳳鳥不至，河不出圖，吾已矣夫！」

子畏于匡。曰：「文王既没，文不在兹乎？天之将丧斯文也，后死者不得与于斯文也；天之未丧斯文也，匡人其如予何？」

大宰问于子贡曰：「夫子圣者与？何其多能也？」子贡曰：「固天纵之将圣，又多能也。」子闻之，曰：「大宰知我乎！吾少也贱，故多能鄙事。君子多乎哉？不多也。」

牢曰：「子云，『吾不试，故艺』。」

子曰：「吾有知乎哉？无知也。有鄙夫问于我，空空如也，我叩其两端而竭焉。」

子曰：「凤鸟不至，河不出图，吾已矣夫！」

CHAP. V. 1. The Master was put in fear in K'wang. 2. He said, 'After the death of King Wan, was not the cause of truth lodged here in me? 3. 'If Heaven had wished to let this cause of truth perish, then I, a future mortal, should not have got such a relation to that cause. While Heaven does not let the cause of truth perish, what can the people of K'wang do to me?'

CHAP. VI. 1. A high officer asked Tsze-kung, saying, 'May we not say that your Master is a sage? How various is his ability!' 2. Tsze-kung said, 'Certainly Heaven has endowed him unlimitedly. He is about a sage. And, moreover, his ability is various.' 3. The Master heard of the conversation and said, 'Does the high officer know me? When I was young, my condition was low, and therefore I acquired my ability in many things, but they were mean matters. Must the superior man have such variety of ability? He does not need variety of ability.' 4. Lao said, 'The Master said, "Having no official employment, I acquired many arts."'

CHAP. VII. The Master said, 'Am I indeed possessed of knowledge? I am not knowing. But if a mean person, who appears quite empty-like, ask anything of me, I set it forth from one end to the other, and exhaust it.'

CHAP. VIII. The Master said, 'The FANG bird does not come; the river sends forth no map:— it is all over with me!'

SEAL SCRIPT

子見齊衰者、冕衣裳者與瞽者，見之，雖少必作；過之，必趨。

顏淵喟然歎曰：「仰之彌高，鑽之彌堅；瞻之在前，忽焉在後。夫子循循然善誘人，博我以文，約我以禮。欲罷不能，既竭吾才，如有所立卓爾。雖欲從之，末由也已。」

子疾病，子路使門人為臣。病閒，曰：「久矣哉！由之行詐也，無臣而為有臣。吾誰欺？欺天乎？且予與其死於臣之手也，無寧死於二三子之手乎？且予縱不得大葬，予死於道路乎？」

子见齐衰者、冕衣裳者与瞽者，见之，虽少必作；过之，必趋。

颜渊喟然叹曰：「仰之弥高，钻之弥坚；瞻之在前，忽焉在后。夫子循循然善诱人，博我以文，约我以礼。欲罢不能，既竭吾才，如有所立卓尔。虽欲从之，末由也已。」

子疾病，子路使门人为臣。病闲，曰：「久矣哉！由之行诈也，无臣而为有臣。吾谁欺？欺天乎？且予与其死于臣之手也，无宁死于二三子之手乎？且予纵不得大葬，予死于道路乎？」

CHAP. IX. When the Master saw a person in a mourning dress, or any one with the cap and upper and lower garments of full dress, or a blind person, on observing them approaching, though they were younger than himself, he would rise up, and if he had to pass by them, he would do so hastily.

CHAP. X. 1. Yen Yuan, in admiration of the Master's doctrines, sighed and said, 'I looked up to them, and they seemed to become more high; I tried to penetrate them, and they seemed to become more firm; I looked at them before me, and suddenly they seemed to be behind. 2. 'The Master, by orderly method, skilfully leads men on. He enlarged my mind with learning, and taught me the restraints of propriety. 3. 'When I wish to give over the study of his doctrines, I cannot do so, and having exerted all my ability, there seems something to stand right up before me; but though I wish to follow and lay hold of it, I really find no way to do so.'

CHAP. XI. 1. The Master being very ill, Tsze-lu wished the disciples to act as ministers to him. 2. During a remission of his illness, he said, 'Long has the conduct of Yu been deceitful! By pretending to have ministers when I have them not, whom should I impose upon? Should I impose upon Heaven? 3. 'Moreover, than that I should die in the hands of ministers, is it not better that I should die in the hands of you, my disciples? And though I may not get a great burial, shall I die upon the road?'

SEAL SCRIPT

子貢曰：「有美玉於斯，韞匵而藏諸？求善賈而沽諸？」子曰：「沽之哉！沽之哉！我待賈者也。」

子欲居九夷。或曰：「陋，如之何！」子曰：「君子居之，何陋之有？」

子曰：「吾自衛反魯，然後樂正，雅頌各得其所。」

子曰：「出則事公卿，入則事父兄，喪事不敢不勉，不為酒困，何有於我哉？」

子在川上，曰：「逝者如斯夫！不舍晝夜。」

子曰：「吾未見好德如好色者也。」

子贡曰：「有美玉于斯，韫匵而藏诸？求善贾而沽诸？」子曰：「沽之哉！沽之哉！我待贾者也。」

子欲居九夷。或曰：「陋，如之何！」子曰：「君子居之，何陋之有？」

子曰：「吾自卫反鲁，然后乐正，雅颂各得其所。」

子曰：「出则事公卿，入则事父兄，丧事不敢不勉，不为酒困，何有于我哉？」

子在川上，曰：「逝者如斯夫！不舍昼夜。」

子曰：「吾未见好德如好色者也。」

CHAP. XII. Tsze-kung said, 'There is a beautiful gem here. Should I lay it up in a case and keep it? or should I seek for a good price and sell it?' The Master said, 'Sell it! Sell it! But I would wait for one to offer the price.'

CHAP. XIII. 1. The Master was wishing to go and live among the nine wild tribes of the east. 2. Some one said, 'They are rude. How can you do such a thing?' The Master said, 'If a superior man dwelt among them, what rudeness would there be?'

CHAP. XIV. The Master said, 'I returned from Wei to Lu, and then the music was reformed, and the pieces in the Royal songs and Praise songs all found their proper places.'

CHAP. XV. The Master said, 'Abroad, to serve the high ministers and nobles; at home, to serve one's father and elder brothers; in all duties to the dead, not to dare not to exert one's self; and not to be overcome of wine:— which one of these things do I attain to?'

CHAP. XVI. The Master standing by a stream, said, 'It passes on just like this, not ceasing day or night!'

CHAP. XVII. The Master said, 'I have not seen one who loves virtue as he loves beauty.'

SEAL SCRIPT

　　子曰：「譬如為山，未成一簣，止，吾止也；譬如平地，雖覆一簣，進，吾往也。」

　　子曰：「語之而不惰者，其回也與！」

　　子謂顏淵，曰：「惜乎！吾見其進也，未見其止也。」

　　子曰：「苗而不秀者有矣夫！秀而不實者有矣夫！」

　　子曰：「後生可畏，焉知來者之不如今也？四十、五十而無聞焉，斯亦不足畏也已。」

　　子曰：「譬如为山，未成一篑，止，吾止也；譬如平地，虽覆一篑，进，吾往也。」

　　子曰：「语之而不惰者，其回也与！」

　　子谓颜渊，曰：「惜乎！吾见其进也，未见其止也。」

　　子曰：「苗而不秀者有矣夫！秀而不实者有矣夫！」

　　子曰：「后生可畏，焉知来者之不如今也？四十、五十而无闻焉，斯亦不足畏也已。」

CHAP. XVIII. The Master said, 'The prosecution of learning may be compared to what may happen in raising a mound. If there want but one basket of earth to complete the work, and I stop, the stopping is my own work. It may be compared to throwing down the earth on the level ground. Though but one basketful is thrown at a time, the advancing with it is my own going forward.'

CHAP. XIX. The Master said, 'Never flagging when I set forth anything to him;— ah! that is Hui.'

CHAP. XX. The Master said of Yen Yuan, 'Alas! I saw his constant advance. I never saw him stop in his progress.'

CHAP. XXI. The Master said, 'There are cases in which the blade springs, but the plant does not go on to flower! There are cases where it flowers, but no fruit is subsequently produced!'

CHAP. XXII. The Master said, 'A youth is to be regarded with respect. How do we know that his future will not be equal to our present? If he reach the age of forty or fifty, and has not made himself heard of, then indeed he will not be worth being regarded with respect.'

SEAL SCRIPT

子曰：「法語之言，能無從乎？改之為貴。巽與之言，能無說乎？繹之為貴。說而不繹，從而不改，吾末如之何也已矣。」

子曰：「主忠信，毋友不如己者，過則勿憚改。」

子曰：「三軍可奪帥也，匹夫不可奪志也。」

子曰：「衣敝縕袍，與衣狐貉者立，而不恥者，其由也與？『不忮不求，何用不臧？』」子路終身誦之。子曰：「是道也，何足以臧？」

子曰：「法语之言，能无从乎？改之为贵。巽与之言，能无说乎？绎之为贵。说而不绎，从而不改，吾末如之何也已矣。」

子曰：「主忠信，毋友不如己者，过则勿惮改。」

子曰：「三军可夺帅也，匹夫不可夺志也。」

子曰：「衣敝缊袍，与衣狐貉者立，而不耻者，其由也与？『不忮不求，何用不臧？』」子路终身诵之。子曰：「是道也，何足以臧？」

CHAP. XXV. The Master said, 'Can men refuse to assent to the words of strict admonition? But it is reforming the conduct because of them which is valuable. Can men refuse to be pleased with words of gentle advice? But it is unfolding their aim which is valuable. If a man be pleased with these words, but does not unfold their aim, and assents to those, but does not reform his conduct, I can really do nothing with him.'

CHAP. XXIV. The Master said, 'Hold faithfulness and sincerity as first principles. Have no friends not equal to yourself. When you have faults, do not fear to abandon them.'

CHAP. XXV. The Master said, 'The commander of the forces of a large state may be carried off, but the will of even a common man cannot be taken from him.'

CHAP. XXVI. 1. The Master said, 'Dressed himself in a tattered robe quilted with hemp, yet standing by the side of men dressed in furs, and not ashamed;— ah! it is Yu who is equal to this! 2. '"He dislikes none, he covets nothing;— what can he do but what is good!"' 3. Tsze-lu kept continually repeating these words of the ode, when the Master said, 'Those things are by no means sufficient to constitute (perfect) excellence.'

SEAL SCRIPT

子曰：「歲寒，然後知松柏之後彫也。」

子曰：「知者不惑，仁者不憂，勇者不懼。」

子曰：「可與共學，未可與適道；可與適道，未可與立；可與立，未可與權。」

「唐棣之華，偏其反而。豈不爾思？室是遠而。」子曰：「未之思也，夫何遠之有？」

子曰：「岁寒，然后知松柏之后雕也。」

子曰：「知者不惑，仁者不忧，勇者不惧。」

子曰：「可与共学，未可与适道；可与适道，未可与立；可与立，未可与权。」

「唐棣之华，偏其反而。岂不尔思？室是远而。」子曰：「未之思也，夫何远之有？」

CHAP. XXVII. The Master said, 'When the year becomes cold, then we know how the pine and the cypress are the last to lose their leaves.'

CHAP. XXVIII. The Master said, 'The wise are free from perplexities; the virtuous from anxiety; and the bold from fear.'

CHAP. XXIX. The Master said, 'There are some with whom we may study in common, but we shall find them unable to go along with us to principles. Perhaps we may go on with them to principles, but we shall find them unable to get established in those along with us. Or if we may get so established along with them, we shall find them unable to weigh occurring events along with us.'

CHAP. XXX. 1. How the flowers of the aspen-plum flutter and turn! Do I not think of you? But your house is distant. 2. The Master said, 'It is the want of thought about it. How is it distant?'

SEAL SCRIPT

鄉黨第十

孔子於鄉黨,恂恂如也,似不能言者。其在宗廟朝廷,便便言,唯謹爾。

朝,與下大夫言,侃侃如也;與上大夫言,誾誾如也。君在,踧踖如也。與與如也。

君召使擯,色勃如也,足躩如也。揖所與立,左右手。衣前後,襜如也。趨進,翼如也。賓退,必復命曰:「賓不顧矣。」

乡党第十

孔子于乡党,恂恂如也,似不能言者。其在宗庙朝廷,便便言,唯谨尔。

朝,与下大夫言,侃侃如也;与上大夫言,訚訚如也。君在,踧踖如也。与与如也。

君召使摈,色勃如也,足躩如也。揖所与立,左右手。衣前后,襜如也。趋进,翼如也。宾退,必复命曰:「宾不顾矣。」

BOOK X. HEANG TANG.

CHAP. I. 1. Confucius, in his village, looked simple and sincere, and as if he were not able to speak. 2. When he was in the prince's ancestorial temple, or in the court, he spoke minutely on every point, but cautiously. CHAP II. 1. When he was waiting at court, in speaking with the great officers of the lower grade, he spake freely, but in a straightforward manner; in speaking with those of the higher grade, he did so blandly, but precisely. 2. When the ruler was present, his manner displayed respectful uneasiness; it was grave, but self-possessed.

CHAP. III. 1. When the prince called him to employ him in the reception of a visitor, his countenance appeared to change, and his legs to move forward with difficulty. 2. He inclined himself to the other officers among whom he stood, moving his left or right arm, as their position required, but keeping the skirts of his robe before and behind evenly adjusted. 3. He hastened forward, with his arms like the wings of a bird. 4. When the guest had retired, he would report to the prince, 'The visitor is not turning round any more.'

SEAL SCRIPT

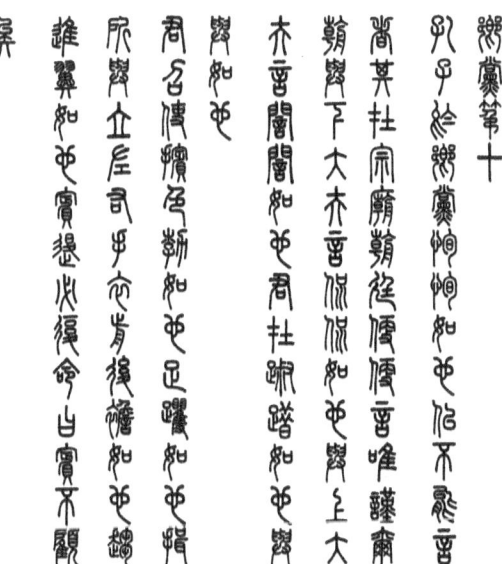

入公門，鞠躬如也，如不容。立不中門，行不履閾。過位，色勃如也，足躩如也，其言似不足者。攝齊升堂，鞠躬如也，屏氣似不息者。出，降一等，逞顏色，怡怡如也。沒階趨進，翼如也。復其位，踧踖如也。

執圭，鞠躬如也，如不勝。上如揖，下如授。勃如戰色，足蹜蹜，如有循。享禮，有容色。私覿，愉愉如也。

入公门，鞠躬如也，如不容。立不中门，行不履阈。过位，色勃如也，足躩如也，其言似不足者。摄齐升堂，鞠躬如也，屏气似不息者。出，降一等，逞颜色，怡怡如也。没阶趋进，翼如也。复其位，踧踖如也。

执圭，鞠躬如也，如不胜。上如揖，下如授。勃如战色，足蹜蹜，如有循。享礼，有容色。私觌，愉愉如也。

CHAP. IV. 1. When he entered the palace gate, he seemed to bend his body, as if it were not sufficient to admit him. 2. When he was standing, he did not occupy the middle of the gate-way; when he passed in or out, he did not tread upon the threshold. 3. When he was passing the vacant place of the prince, his countenance appeared to change, and his legs to bend under him, and his words came as if he hardly had breath to utter them. 4. He ascended the reception hall, holding up his robe with both his hands, and his body bent; holding in his breath also, as if he dared not breathe. 5. When he came out from the audience, as soon as he had descended one step, he began to relax his countenance, and had a satisfied look. When he had got to the bottom of the steps, he advanced rapidly to his place, with his arms like wings, and on occupying it, his manner still showed respectful uneasiness.

CHAP. V. 1. When he was carrying the scepter of his ruler, he seemed to bend his body, as if he were not able to bear its weight. He did not hold it higher than the position of the hands in making a bow, nor lower than their position in giving anything to another. His countenance seemed to change, and look apprehensive, and he dragged his feet along as if they were held by something to the ground. 2. In presenting the presents with which he was charged, he wore a placid appearance. 3. At his private audience, he looked highly pleased.

SEAL SCRIPT

君子不以紺緅飾。紅紫不以為褻服。當暑，袗絺綌，必表而出之。緇衣羔裘，素衣麑裘，黃衣狐裘。褻裘長。短右袂。必有寢衣，長一身有半。狐貉之厚以居。去喪，無所不佩。非帷裳，必殺之。羔裘玄冠不以吊。吉月，必朝服而朝。

齊，必有明衣，布。齊，必變食，居必遷坐。

君子不以绀緅饰。红紫不以为亵服。当暑，袗绤绤，必表而出之。缁衣羔裘，素衣麑裘，黄衣狐裘。亵裘长。短右袂。必有寝衣，长一身有半。狐貉之厚以居。去丧，无所不佩。非帷裳，必杀之。羔裘玄冠不以吊。吉月，必朝服而朝。

齐，必有明衣，布。齐，必变食，居必迁坐。

CHAP. VI. 1. The superior man did not use a deep purple, or a puce colour, in the ornaments of his dress. 2. Even in his undress, he did not wear anything of a red or reddish colour. 3. In warm weather, he had a single garment either of coarse or fine texture, but he wore it displayed over an inner garment. 4. Over lamb's fur he wore a garment of black; over fawn's fur one of white; and over fox's fur one of yellow. 5. The fur robe of his undress was long, with the right sleeve short. 6. He required his sleeping dress to be half as long again as his body. 7. When staying at home, he used thick furs of the fox or the badger. 8. When he put off mourning, he wore all the appendages of the girdle. 9. His under-garment, except when it was required to be of the curtain shape, was made of silk cut narrow above and wide below. 10. He did not wear lamb's fur or a black cap, on a visit of condolence. 11. On the first day of the month he put on his court robes, and presented himself at court.

CHAP. VII. 1. When fasting, he thought it necessary to have his clothes brightly clean and made of linen cloth. 2. When fasting, he thought it necessary to change his food, and also to change the place where he commonly sat in the apartment.

SEAL SCRIPT

食不厭精，膾不厭細。食饐而餲，魚餒而肉敗，不食。色惡，不食。臭惡，不食。失飪，不食。不時，不食。割不正，不食。不得其醬，不食。肉雖多，不使勝食氣。惟酒無量，不及亂。沽酒市脯不食。不撤薑食。不多食。祭於公，不宿肉。祭肉不出三日。出三日，不食之矣。食不語，寢不言。雖疏食菜羹，瓜祭，必齊如也。

席不正，不坐。

食不厌精，脍不厌细。食饐而餲，鱼馁而肉败，不食。色恶，不食。臭恶，不食。失饪，不食。不时，不食。割不正，不食。不得其酱，不食。肉虽多，不使胜食气。惟酒无量，不及乱。沽酒市脯不食。不撤姜食。不多食。祭于公，不宿肉。祭肉不出三日。出三日，不食之矣。食不语，寝不言。虽疏食菜羹，瓜祭，必齐如也。

席不正，不坐。

CHAP. VIII. 1. He did not dislike to have his rice finely cleaned, nor to have his minced meat cut quite small. 2. He did not eat rice which had been injured by heat or damp and turned sour, nor fish or flesh which was gone. He did not eat what was discoloured, or what was of a bad flavour, nor anything which was ill-cooked, or was not in season. 3. He did not eat meat which was not cut properly, nor what was served without its proper sauce. 4. Though there might be a large quantity of meat, he would not allow what he took to exceed the due proportion for the rice. It was only in wine that he laid down no limit for himself, but he did not allow himself to be confused by it. 5. He did not partake of wine and dried meat bought in the market. 6. He was never without ginger when he ate. 7. He did not eat much. 8. When he had been assisting at the prince's sacrifice, he did not keep the flesh which he received overnight. The flesh of his family sacrifice he did not keep over three days. If kept over three days, people could not eat it. 9. When eating, he did not converse. When in bed, he did not speak. 10. Although his food might be coarse rice and vegetable soup, he would offer a little of it in sacrifice with a grave, respectful air.

CHAP. IX. If his mat was not straight, he did not sit on it.

SEAL SCRIPT

　　鄉人飲酒，杖者出，斯出矣。鄉人儺，朝服而立於阼階。

　　問人於他邦，再拜而送之。康子饋藥，拜而受之。曰：「丘未達，不敢嘗。」

　　廐焚。子退朝，曰：「傷人乎？」不問馬。

　　君賜食，必正席先嘗之；君賜腥，必熟而薦之；君賜生，必畜之。侍食於君，君祭，先飯。疾，君視之，東首，加朝服，拖紳。君命召，不俟駕行矣。

　　乡人饮酒，杖者出，斯出矣。乡人傩，朝服而立于阼阶。

　　问人于他邦，再拜而送之。康子馈药，拜而受之。曰：「丘未达，不敢尝。」

　　厩焚。子退朝，曰：「伤人乎？」不问马。

　　君赐食，必正席先尝之；君赐腥，必熟而荐之；君赐生，必畜之。侍食于君，君祭，先饭。疾，君视之，东首，加朝服，拖绅。君命召，不俟驾行矣。

CHAP. X. 1. When the villagers were drinking together, on those who carried staffs going out, he went out immediately after. 2. When the villagers were going through their ceremonies to drive away pestilential influences, he put on his court robes and stood on the eastern steps.

CHAP. XI. 1. When he was sending complimentary inquiries to any one in another State, he bowed twice as he escorted the messenger away. 2. Chi K'ang having sent him a present of physic, he bowed and received it, saying, 'I do not know it. I dare not taste it.'

CHAP. XII. The stable being burned down, when he was at court, on his return he said, 'Has any man been hurt?' He did not ask about the horses.

CHAP. XIII. 1. When the prince sent him a gift of cooked meat, he would adjust his mat, first taste it, and then give it away to others. When the prince sent him a gift of undressed meat, he would have it cooked, and offer it to the spirits of his ancestors. When the prince sent him a gift of a living animal, he would keep it alive. 2. When he was in attendance on the prince and joining in the entertainment, the prince only sacrificed. He first tasted everything. 3. When he was ill and the prince came to visit him, he had his head to the east, made his court robes be spread over him, and drew his girdle across them. 4. When the prince's order called him, without waiting for his carriage to be yoked, he went at once.

SEAL SCRIPT

123

入太廟，每事問。

朋友死，無所歸。曰：「於我殯。」朋友之饋，雖車馬，非祭肉，不拜。

寢不尸，居不容。見齊衰者，雖狎，必變。見冕者與瞽者，雖褻，必以貌。凶服者式之。式負版者。有盛饌，必變色而作。迅雷風烈，必變。

入太庙，每事问。

朋友死，无所归。曰：「于我殡。」朋友之馈，虽车马，非祭肉，不拜。

寝不尸，居不容。见齐衰者，虽狎，必变。见冕者与瞽者，虽亵，必以貌。凶服者式之。式负版者。有盛馔，必变色而作。迅雷风烈，必变。

CHAP. XIV. When he entered the ancestral temple of the State, he asked about everything.

CHAP. XV. 1. When any of his friends died, if he had no relations who could be depended on for the necessary offices, he would say, 'I will bury him.' 2. When a friend sent him a present, though it might be a carriage and horses, he did not bow. 3. The only present for which he bowed was that of the flesh of sacrifice.

CHAP. XVI. 1. In bed, he did not lie like a corpse. At home, he did not put on any formal deportment. 2. When he saw any one in a mourning dress, though it might be an acquaintance, he would change countenance; when he saw any one wearing the cap of full dress, or a blind person, though he might be in his undress, he would salute them in a ceremonious manner. 3. To any person in mourning he bowed forward to the crossbar of his carriage; he bowed in the same way to any one bearing the tables of population. 4. When he was at an entertainment where there was an abundance of provisions set before him, he would change countenance and rise up. 5. On a sudden clap of thunder, or a violent wind, he would change countenance.

SEAL SCRIPT

升車，必正立執綏。車中，不內顧，不疾言，不親指。

色斯舉矣，翔而後集。曰：「山梁雌雉，時哉！時哉！」子路共之，三嗅而作。

升车，必正立执绥。车中，不内顾，不疾言，不亲指。

色斯举矣，翔而后集。曰：「山梁雌雉，时哉！时哉！」子路共之，三嗅而作。

CHAP. XVII. 1. When he was about to mount his carriage, he would stand straight, holding the cord. 2. When he was in the carriage, he did not turn his head quite round, he did not talk hastily, he did not point with his hands.

CHAP. XVIII. 1. Seeing the countenance, it instantly rises. It flies round, and by and by settles. 2. The Master said, 'There is the hen-pheasant on the hill bridge. At its season! At its season!' Tsze-lu made a motion to it. Thrice it smelt him and then rose.

SEAL SCRIPT

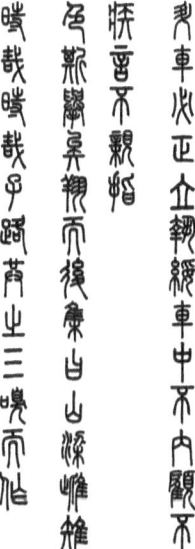

先進第十一

子曰：「先進於禮樂，野人也；後進於禮樂，君子也。如用之，則吾從先進。」

子曰：「從我於陳、蔡者，皆不及門也。」

德行：顏淵，閔子騫，冉伯牛，仲弓。言語：宰我，子貢。政事：冉有，季路。文學：子游，子夏。

子曰：「回也非助我者也，於吾言無所不說。」

子曰：「孝哉閔子騫！人不間於其父母昆弟之言。」

先进第十一

子曰：「先进于礼乐，野人也；后进于礼乐，君子也。如用之，则吾从先进。」

子曰：「从我于陈、蔡者，皆不及门也。」

德行：颜渊，闵子骞，冉伯牛，仲弓。言语：宰我，子贡。政事：冉有，季路。文学：子游，子夏。

子曰：「回也非助我者也，于吾言无所不说。」

子曰：「孝哉闵子骞！人不间于其父母昆弟之言。」

BOOK XI. HSIEN TSIN.

CHAP. I. 1. The Master said, 'The men of former times, in the matters of ceremonies and music were rustics, it is said, while the men of these latter times, in ceremonies and music, are accomplished gentlemen. 2. 'If I have occasion to use those things, I follow the men of former times.'

CHAP. II. 1. The Master said, 'Of those who were with me in Ch'an and Ts'ai, there are none to be found to enter my door.' 2. Distinguished for their virtuous principles and practice, there were Yen Yuan, Min Tsze-ch'ien, Zan Po-niu, and Chung-kung; for their ability in speech, Tsai Wo and Tsze-kung; for their administrative talents, Zan Yu and Chi Lu; for their literary acquirements, Tsze-yu and Tsze-hsia.

CHAP. III. The Master said, 'Hui gives me no assistance. There is nothing that I say in which he does not delight.'

CHAP. IV. The Master said, 'Filial indeed is Min Tsze-ch'ien! Other people say nothing of him different from the report of his parents and brothers.'

SEAL SCRIPT

南容三復白圭，孔子以其兄之子妻之。

季康子問：「弟子孰為好學？」孔子對曰：「有顏回者好學，不幸短命死矣！今也則亡。」

顏淵死，顏路請子之車以為之槨。子曰：「才不才，亦各言其子也。鯉也死，有棺而無槨。吾不徒行以為之槨。以吾從大夫之後，不可徒行也。」

顏淵死。子曰：「噫！天喪予！天喪予！」

顏淵死，子哭之慟。從者曰：「子慟矣。」曰：「有慟乎？非夫人之為慟而誰為！」

南容三复白圭，孔子以其兄之子妻之。

季康子问：「弟子孰为好学？」孔子对曰：「有颜回者好学，不幸短命死矣！今也则亡。」

颜渊死，颜路请子之车以为之椁。子曰：「才不才，亦各言其子也。鲤也死，有棺而无椁。吾不徒行以为之椁。以吾从大夫之后，不可徒行也。」

颜渊死。子曰：「噫！天丧予！天丧予！」

颜渊死，子哭之恸。从者曰：「子恸矣。」曰：「有恸乎？非夫人之为恸而谁为！」

CHAP. V. Nan Yung was frequently repeating the lines about a white scepter stone. Confucius gave him the daughter of his elder brother to wife.

CHAP. VI. Chi K'ang asked which of the disciples loved to learn. Confucius replied to him, 'There was Yen Hui; he loved to learn. Unfortunately his appointed time was short, and he died. Now there is no one who loves to learn, as he did.'

CHAP. VII. 1. When Yen Yuan died, Yen Lu begged the carriage of the Master to sell and get an outer shell for his son's coffin. 2. The Master said, 'Every one calls his son his son, whether he has talents or has not talents. There was Li; when he died, he had a coffin but no outer shell. I would not walk on foot to get a shell for him, because, having followed in the rear of the great officers, it was not proper that I should walk on foot.'

CHAP. VIII. When Yen Yuan died, the Master said, 'Alas! Heaven is destroying me! Heaven is destroying me!'

CHAP. IX. 1. When Yen Yuan died, the Master bewailed him exceedingly, and the disciples who were with him said, 'Master, your grief is excessive?' 2. 'Is it excessive?' said he. 3. 'If I am not to mourn bitterly for this man, for whom should I mourn?'

SEAL SCRIPT

　　顏淵死，門人欲厚葬之，子曰：「不可。」門人厚葬之。子曰：「回也視予猶父也，予不得視猶子也。非我也，夫二三子也。」

　　季路問事鬼神。子曰：「未能事人，焉能事鬼？」敢問死。曰：「未知生，焉知死？」

　　閔子侍側，誾誾如也；子路，行行如也；冉有、子貢，侃侃如也。子樂。「若由也，不得其死然。」

　　魯人為長府。閔子騫曰：「仍舊貫，如之何？何必改作？」子曰：「夫人不言，言必有中。」

　　颜渊死，门人欲厚葬之，子曰：「不可。」门人厚葬之。子曰：「回也视予犹父也，予不得视犹子也。非我也，夫二三子也。」

　　季路问事鬼神。子曰：「未能事人，焉能事鬼？」敢问死。曰：「未知生，焉知死？」

　　闵子侍侧，訚訚如也；子路，行行如也；冉有、子贡，侃侃如也。子乐。「若由也，不得其死然。」

　　鲁人为长府。闵子骞曰：「仍旧贯，如之何？何必改作？」子曰：「夫人不言，言必有中。」

CHAP. X. 1. When Yen Yuan died, the disciples wished to give him a great funeral, and the Master said, 'You may not do so.' 2. The disciples did bury him in great style. 3. The Master said, 'Hui behaved towards me as his father. I have not been able to treat him as my son. The fault is not mine; it belongs to you, O disciples.'

CHAP. XI. Chi Lu asked about serving the spirits of the dead. The Master said, 'While you are not able to serve men, how can you serve their spirits?' Chi Lu added, 'I venture to ask about death?' He was answered, 'While you do not know life, how can you know about death?'

CHAP. XII. 1. The disciple Min was standing by his side, looking bland and precise; Tsze-lu, looking bold and soldierly; Zan Yu and Tsze-kung, with a free and straightforward manner. The Master was pleased. 2. He said, 'Yu, there!— he will not die a natural death.'

CHAP. XIII. 1. Some parties in Lu were going to take down and rebuild the Long Treasury. 2. Min Tsze-ch'ien said, 'Suppose it were to be repaired after its old style;— why must it be altered and made anew?' 3. The Master said, 'This man seldom speaks; when he does, he is sure to hit the point.'

SEAL SCRIPT

子曰：「由之瑟奚為於丘之門？」門人不敬子路。子曰：「由也升堂矣，未入於室也。」

子貢問：「師與商也孰賢？」子曰：「師也過，商也不及。」曰：「然則師愈與？」子曰：「過猶不及。」

季氏富於周公，而求也為之聚斂而附益之。子曰：「非吾徒也。小子鳴鼓而攻之，可也。」

柴也愚，參也魯，師也辟，由也喭。

子曰：「回也其庶乎，屢空。賜不受命，而貨殖焉，億則屢中。」

子曰：「由之瑟奚为于丘之门？」门人不敬子路。子曰：「由也升堂矣，未入于室也。」

子贡问：「师与商也孰贤？」子曰：「师也过，商也不及。」曰：「然则师愈与？」子曰：「过犹不及。」

季氏富于周公，而求也为之聚敛而附益之。子曰：「非吾徒也。小子鸣鼓而攻之，可也。」

柴也愚，参也鲁，师也辟，由也喭。

子曰：「回也其庶乎，屡空。赐不受命，而货殖焉，亿则屡中。」

CHAP. XIV. 1. The Master said, 'What has the lute of Yu to do in my door?'
2. The other disciples began not to respect Tsze-lu. The Master said, 'Yu has
ascended to the hall, though he has not yet passed into the inner apartments.'

CHAP. XV. 1. Tsze-kung asked which of the two, Shih or Shang, was the
superior. The Master said, 'Shih goes beyond the due mean, and Shang does not
come up to it.' 2. 'Then,' said Tsze-kung, 'the superiority is with Shih, I suppose.'
3. The Master said, 'To go beyond is as wrong as to fall short.'

CHAP. XVI. 1. The head of the Chi family was richer than the duke of Chau
had been, and yet Ch'iu collected his imposts for him, and increased his wealth. 2.
The Master said, 'He is no disciple of mine. My little children, beat the drum and
assail him.'

CHAP. XVII. 1. Ch'ai is simple. 2. Shan is dull. 3. Shih is specious. 4. Yu is
coarse.

CHAP. XVIII. 1. The Master said, 'There is Hui! He has nearly attained to
perfect virtue. He is often in want. 2. 'Ts'ze does not acquiesce in the appointments of Heaven, and his goods are increased by him. Yet his judgments are often
correct.'

SEAL SCRIPT

子張問善人之道。子曰：「不踐跡，亦不入於室。」

子曰：「論篤是與，君子者乎？色莊者乎？」

子路問：「聞斯行諸？」子曰：「有父兄在，如之何其聞斯行之？」冉有問：「聞斯行諸？」子曰：「聞斯行之。」公西華曰：「由也問聞斯行諸，子曰『有父兄在』；求也問聞斯行諸，子曰『聞斯行之』。赤也惑，敢問。」子曰：「求也退，故進之；由也兼人，故退之。」

子张问善人之道。子曰：「不践迹，亦不入于室。」

子曰：「论笃是与，君子者乎？色庄者乎？」

子路问：「闻斯行诸？」子曰：「有父兄在，如之何其闻斯行之？」冉有问：「闻斯行诸？」子曰：「闻斯行之。」公西华曰：「由也问闻斯行诸，子曰『有父兄在』；求也问闻斯行诸，子曰『闻斯行之』。赤也惑，敢问。」子曰：「求也退，故进之；由也兼人，故退之。」

CHAP. XIX. Tsze-chang asked what were the characteristics of the GOOD man. The Master said, 'He does not tread in the footsteps of others, but moreover, he does not enter the chamber of the sage.'

CHAP. XX. The Master said, 'If, because a man's discourse appears solid and sincere, we allow him to be a good man, is he really a superior man? or is his gravity only in appearance?'

CHAP. XXI. Tsze-lu asked whether he should immediately carry into practice what he heard. The Master said, 'There are your father and elder brothers to be consulted;— why should you act on that principle of immediately carrying into practice what you hear?' Zan Yu asked the same, whether he should immediately carry into practice what he heard, and the Master answered, 'Immediately carry into practice what you hear.' Kung-hsi Hwa said, 'Yu asked whether he should carry immediately into practice what he heard, and you said, "There are your father and elder brothers to be consulted." Ch'iu asked whether he should immediately carry into practice what he heard, and you said, "Carry it immediately into practice." I, Ch'ih, am perplexed, and venture to ask you for an explanation.' The Master said, 'Ch'iu is retiring and slow; therefore, I urged him forward. Yu has more than his own share of energy; therefore I kept him back.'

SEAL SCRIPT

137

子畏於匡，顏淵後。子曰：「吾以女為死矣。」曰：「子在，回何敢死？」

季子然問：「仲由、冉求可謂大臣與？」子曰：「吾以子為異之問，曾由與求之問。所謂大臣者：以道事君，不可則止。今由與求也，可謂具臣矣。」曰：「然則從之者與？」子曰：「弒父與君，亦不從也。」

子畏于匡，颜渊后。子曰：「吾以女为死矣。」曰：「子在，回何敢死？」

季子然问：「仲由、冉求可谓大臣与？」子曰：「吾以子为异之问，曾由与求之问。所谓大臣者：以道事君，不可则止。今由与求也，可谓具臣矣。」曰：「然则从之者与？」子曰：「弒父与君，亦不从也。」

CHAP. XXII. The Master was put in fear in K'wang and Yen Yuan fell behind. The Master, on his rejoining him, said, 'I thought you had died.' Hui replied, 'While you were alive, how should I presume to die?'

CHAP. XXIII. 1. Chi Tsze-zan asked whether Chung Yu and Zan Ch'iu could be called great ministers. 2. The Master said, 'I thought you would ask about some extraordinary individuals, and you only ask about Yu and Ch'iu! 3. 'What is called a great minister, is one who serves his prince according to what is right, and when he finds he cannot do so, retires. 4. 'Now, as to Yu and Ch'iu, they may be called ordinary ministers.' 5. Tsze-zan said, 'Then they will always follow their chief;—will they?' 6. The Master said, 'In an act of parricide or regicide, they would not follow him.'

SEAL SCRIPT

子路使子羔為費宰。子曰：「賊夫人之子。」子路曰：「有民人焉，有社稷焉。何必讀書，然後為學？」子曰：「是故惡夫佞者。」

子路使子羔为费宰。子曰：「贼夫人之子。」子路曰：「有民人焉，有社稷焉。何必读书，然后为学？」子曰：「是故恶夫佞者。」

CHAP. XXIV. 1. Tsze-lu got Tsze-kao appointed governor of Pi. 2. The Master said, 'You are injuring a man's son.' 3. Tsze-lu said, 'There are (there) common people and officers; there are the altars of the spirits of the land and grain. Why must one read books before he can be considered to have learned?' 4. The Master said, 'It is on this account that I hate your glib-tongued people.'

SEAL SCRIPT

　　子路、曾皙、冉有、公西華侍坐。子曰：「以吾一日長乎爾，毋吾以也。居則曰：『不吾知也！』如或知爾，則何以哉？」子路率爾而對曰：「千乘之國，攝乎大國之間，加之以師旅，因之以饑饉；由也為之，比及三年，可使有勇，且知方也。」夫子哂之。「求！爾何如？」對曰：「方六七十，如五六十，求也為之，比及三年，可使足民。如其禮樂，以俟君子。」「赤！爾何如？」對曰：「非曰能之，願學焉。宗廟之事，如會同，端章甫，願為小相焉。」「點！爾何如？」鼓瑟希，鏗爾，舍瑟而作。對曰：「異乎三子者之撰。」子曰：「何傷乎？亦各言其志也。」曰：「莫春者，春服既成。冠者五六人，童子六七人，浴乎沂，風乎舞雩，詠而歸。」夫子喟然歎曰：「吾與點也！」三子者出，曾皙後。曾皙曰：「夫三子者之言何如？」子曰：「亦各言其志也已矣。」曰：「夫子何哂由也？」曰：「為國以禮，其言不讓，是故哂之。」「唯求則非

　　子路、曾皙、冉有、公西华侍坐。子曰：「以吾一日长乎尔，毋吾以也。居则曰：『不吾知也！』如或知尔，则何以哉？」子路率尔而对曰：「千乘之国，摄乎大国之间，加之以师旅，因之以饥馑；由也为之，比及三年，可使有勇，且知方也。」夫子哂之。「求！尔何如？」对曰：「方六七十，如五六十，求也为之，比及三年，可使足民。如其礼乐，以俟君子。」「赤！尔何如？」对曰：「非曰能之，愿学焉。宗庙之事，如会同，端章甫，愿为小相焉。」「点！尔何如？」鼓瑟希，铿尔，舍瑟而作。对曰：「异乎三子者之撰。」子曰：「何伤乎？亦各言其志也。」曰：「莫春者，春服既成。冠者五六人，童子六七人，浴乎沂，风乎舞雩，咏而归。」夫子喟然叹曰：「吾与点也！」三子者出，曾皙后。曾皙曰：「夫三子者之言何如？」子曰：「亦各言其志也已矣。」曰：「夫子何哂由也？」曰：「为国以礼，其言不让，是故哂之。」「唯求则非

CHAP. XXV. 1. Tsze-lu, Tsang Hsi, Zan Yu, and Kung-hsi Hwa were sitting by the Master. 2. He said to them, 'Though I am a day or so older than you, do not think of that. 3. 'From day to day you are saying, "We are not known." If some ruler were to know you, what would you like to do?' 4. Tsze-lu hastily and lightly replied, 'Suppose the case of a State of ten thousand chariots; let it be straitened between other large States; let it be suffering from invading armies; and to this let there be added a famine in corn and in all vegetables:— if I were intrusted with the government of it, in three years' time I could make the people to be bold, and to recognise the rules of righteous conduct.' The Master smiled at him. 5. Turning to Yen Yu, he said, 'Ch'iu, what are your wishes?' Ch'iu replied, 'Suppose a state of sixty or seventy li square, or one of fifty or sixty, and let me have the government of it;— in three years' time, I could make plenty to abound among the people. As to teaching them the principles of propriety, and music, I must wait for the rise of a superior man to do that.' 6. 'What are your wishes, Ch'ih,' said the Master next to Kung- hsi Hwa. Ch'ih replied, 'I do not say that my ability extends to these things, but I should wish to learn them. At the services of the ancestral temple, and at the audiences of the princes with the sovereign, I should like, dressed in the dark square-made robe and the black linen cap, to act as a small assistant.' 7. Last of all, the Master asked Tsang Hsi, 'Tien, what are your wishes?' Tien, pausing as he was playing on his lute, while it was yet twang-

SEAL SCRIPT

邦也與?」「安見方六七十如五六十而非邦也者?」「唯赤則非
邦也與?」「宗廟會同,非諸侯而何?赤也為之小,孰能為之大?」

邦也与?」「安见方六七十如五六十而非邦也者?」「唯赤则非
邦也与?」「宗庙会同,非诸侯而何?赤也为之小,孰能为之大?」

ing, laid the instrument aside, and rose. 'My wishes,' he said, 'are different from the cherished purposes of these three gentlemen.' 'What harm is there in that?' said the Master; 'do you also, as well as they, speak out your wishes.' Tien then said, 'In this, the last month of spring, with the dress of the season all complete, along with five or six young men who have assumed the cap, and six or seven boys, I would wash in the I, enjoy the breeze among the rain altars, and return home singing.' The Master heaved a sigh and said, 'I give my approval to Tien.' 8. The three others having gone out, Tsang Hsi remained behind, and said, 'What do you think of the words of these three friends?' The Master replied, 'They simply told each one his wishes.' 9. Hsi pursued, 'Master, why did you smile at Yu?' 10. He was answered, 'The management of a State demands the rules of propriety. His words were not humble; therefore I smiled at him.' 11. Hsi again said, 'But was it not a State which Ch'iu proposed for himself?' The reply was, 'Yes; did you ever see a territory of sixty or seventy li or one of fifty or sixty, which was not a State?' 12. Once more, Hsi inquired, 'And was it not a State which Ch'ih proposed for himself?' The Master again replied, 'Yes; who but princes have to do with ancestral temples, and with audiences but the sovereign? If Ch'ih were to be a small assistant in these services, who could be a great one?

SEAL SCRIPT

145

顏淵第十二

　　顏淵問仁。子曰:「克己復禮為仁。一日克己復禮,天下歸仁焉。為仁由己,而由人乎哉?」顏淵曰:「請問其目。」子曰:「非禮勿視,非禮勿聽,非禮勿言,非禮勿動。」顏淵曰:「回雖不敏,請事斯語矣。」

　　仲弓問仁。子曰:「出門如見大賓,使民如承大祭。己所不欲,勿施於人。在邦無怨,在家無怨。」仲弓曰:「雍雖不敏,請事斯語矣。」

颜渊第十二

　　颜渊问仁。子曰:「克己复礼为仁。一日克己复礼,天下归仁焉。为仁由己,而由人乎哉?」颜渊曰:「请问其目。」子曰:「非礼勿视,非礼勿听,非礼勿言,非礼勿动。」颜渊曰:「回虽不敏,请事斯语矣。」

　　仲弓问仁。子曰:「出门如见大宾,使民如承大祭。己所不欲,勿施于人。在邦无怨,在家无怨。」仲弓曰:「雍虽不敏,请事斯语矣。」

BOOK XII. YEN YUAN.

CHAP. I. 1. Yen Yuan asked about perfect virtue. The Master said, 'To subdue one's self and return to propriety, is perfect virtue. If a man can for one day subdue himself and return to propriety, all under heaven will ascribe perfect virtue to him. Is the practice of perfect virtue from a man himself, or is it from others?' 2. Yen Yuan said, 'I beg to ask the steps of that process.' The Master replied, 'Look not at what is contrary to propriety; listen not to what is contrary to propriety; speak not what is contrary to propriety; make no movement which is contrary to propriety.' Yen Yuan then said, 'Though I am deficient in intelligence and vigour, I will make it my business to practise this lesson.'

CHAP. II. Chung-kung asked about perfect virtue. The Master said, 'It is, when you go abroad, to behave to every one as if you were receiving a great guest; to employ the people as if you were assisting at a great sacrifice; not to do to others as you would not wish done to yourself; to have no murmuring against you in the country, and none in the family.' Chung-kung said, 'Though I am deficient in intelligence and vigour, I will make it my business to practise this lesson.'

SEAL SCRIPT

司馬牛問仁。子曰：「仁者其言也訒。」曰：「其言也訒，斯謂之仁已乎？」子曰：「為之難，言之得無訒乎？」

司馬牛問君子。子曰：「君子不憂不懼。」曰：「不憂不懼，斯謂之君子已乎？」子曰：「內省不疚，夫何憂何懼？」

司馬牛憂曰：「人皆有兄弟，我獨亡。」子夏曰：「商聞之矣：死生有命，富貴在天。君子敬而無失，與人恭而有禮。四海之內，皆兄弟也。君子何患乎無兄弟也？」

司马牛问仁。子曰：「仁者其言也讱。」曰：「其言也讱，斯谓之仁已乎？」子曰：「为之难，言之得无讱乎？」

司马牛问君子。子曰：「君子不忧不惧。」曰：「不忧不惧，斯谓之君子已乎？」子曰：「内省不疚，夫何忧何惧？」

司马牛忧曰：「人皆有兄弟，我独亡。」子夏曰：「商闻之矣：死生有命，富贵在天。君子敬而无失，与人恭而有礼。四海之内，皆兄弟也。君子何患乎无兄弟也？」

CHAP. III. 1. Sze-ma Niu asked about perfect virtue. 2. The Master said, 'The man of perfect virtue is cautious and slow in his speech.' 3. 'Cautious and slow in his speech!' said Niu;— 'is this what is meant by perfect virtue?' The Master said, 'When a man feels the difficulty of doing, can he be other than cautious and slow in speaking?'

CHAP. IV. 1. Sze-ma Niu asked about the superior man. The Master said, 'The superior man has neither anxiety nor fear.' 2. 'Being without anxiety or fear!' said Nui;— 'does this constitute what we call the superior man?' 3. The Master said, 'When internal examination discovers nothing wrong, what is there to be anxious about, what is there to fear?'

CHAP. V. 1. Sze-ma Niu, full of anxiety, said, 'Other men all have their brothers, I only have not.' 2. Tsze-hsia said to him, 'There is the following saying which I have heard:— 3. '"Death and life have their determined appointment; riches and honours depend upon Heaven." 4. 'Let the superior man never fail reverentially to order his own conduct, and let him be respectful to others and observant of propriety:— then all within the four seas will be his brothers. What has the superior man to do with being distressed because he has no brothers?'

SEAL SCRIPT

149

　　子張問明。子曰：「浸潤之譖，膚受之愬，不行焉。可謂明也已矣。浸潤之譖膚受之愬不行焉，可謂遠也已矣。」

　　子貢問政。子曰：「足食。足兵。民信之矣。」子貢曰：「必不得已而去，於斯三者何先？」曰：「去兵。」子貢曰：「必不得已而去，於斯二者何先？」曰：「去食。自古皆有死，民無信不立。」

　　子张问明。子曰：「浸润之谮，肤受之愬，不行焉。可谓明也已矣。浸润之谮肤受之愬不行焉，可谓远也已矣。」

　　子贡问政。子曰：「足食。足兵。民信之矣。」子贡曰：「必不得已而去，于斯三者何先？」曰：「去兵。」子贡曰：「必不得已而去，于斯二者何先？」曰：「去食。自古皆有死，民无信不立。」

CHAP. VI. Tsze-chang asked what constituted intelligence. The Master said, 'He with whom neither slander that gradually soaks into the mind, nor statements that startle like a wound in the flesh, are successful, may be called intelligent indeed. Yea, he with whom neither soaking slander, nor startling statements, are successful, may be called farseeing.'

CHAP. VII. 1. Tsze-kung asked about government. The Master said, 'The requisites of government are that there be sufficiency of food, sufficiency of military equipment, and the confidence of the people in their ruler.' 2. Tsze-kung said, 'If it cannot be helped, and one of these must be dispensed with, which of the three should be foregone first?' 'The military equipment,' said the Master. 3. Tsze-kung again asked, 'If it cannot be helped, and one of the remaining two must be dispensed with, which of them should be foregone?' The Master answered, 'Part with the food. From of old, death has been the lot of all men; but if the people have no faith in their rulers, there is no standing for the state.'

SEAL SCRIPT

　　棘子成曰：「君子質而已矣，何以文為？」子貢曰：「惜乎！夫子之說，君子也。駟不及舌。文猶質也，質猶文也。虎豹之鞹，猶犬羊之鞹。」

　　哀公問於有若曰：「年饑，用不足，如之何？」有若對曰：「盍徹乎？」曰：「二，吾猶不足，如之何其徹也？」對曰：「百姓足，君孰與不足？百姓不足，君孰與足？」

　　子張問崇德、辨惑。子曰：「主忠信，徙義，崇德也。愛之欲其生，惡之欲其死。既欲其生，又欲其死，是惑也。『誠不以富，亦祇以異。』」

　　棘子成曰：「君子质而已矣，何以文为？」子贡曰：「惜乎！夫子之说，君子也。驷不及舌。文犹质也，质犹文也。虎豹之鞹，犹犬羊之鞹。」

　　哀公问于有若曰：「年饥，用不足，如之何？」有若对曰：「盍彻乎？」曰：「二，吾犹不足，如之何其彻也？」对曰：「百姓足，君孰与不足？百姓不足，君孰与足？」

　　子张问崇德、辨惑。子曰：「主忠信，徙义，崇德也。爱之欲其生，恶之欲其死。既欲其生，又欲其死，是惑也。『诚不以富，亦祇以异。』」

CHAP. VIII. 1. Chi Tsze-ch'ang said, 'In a superior man it is only the substantial qualities which are wanted;— why should we seek for ornamental accomplishments?' 2. Tsze-kung said, 'Alas! Your words, sir, show you to be a superior man, but four horses cannot overtake the tongue. 3. Ornament is as substance; substance is as ornament. The hide of a tiger or a leopard stripped of its hair, is like the hide of a dog or a goat stripped of its hair.'

CHAP. IX. 1. The Duke Ai inquired of Yu Zo, saying, 'The year is one of scarcity, and the returns for expenditure are not sufficient;— what is to be done?' 2. Yu Zo replied to him, 'Why not simply tithe the people?' 3. 'With two tenths, said the duke, 'I find it not enough;— how could I do with that system of one tenth?' 4. Yu Zo answered, 'If the people have plenty, their prince will not be left to want alone. If the people are in want, their prince cannot enjoy plenty alone.'

CHAP. X. 1. Tsze-chang having asked how virtue was to be exalted, and delusions to be discovered, the Master said, 'Hold faithfulness and sincerity as first principles, and be moving continually to what is right;— this is the way to exalt one's virtue. 2. 'You love a man and wish him to live; you hate him and wish him to die. Having wished him to live, you also wish him to die. This is a case of delusion. 3. '"It may not be on account of her being rich, yet you come to make a difference."'

SEAL SCRIPT

齊景公問政於孔子。孔子對曰:「君君,臣臣,父父,子子。」
公曰:「善哉!信如君不君,臣不臣,父不父,子不子,雖有粟,
吾得而食諸?」
　　子曰:「片言可以折獄者,其由也與?」子路無宿諾。
　　子曰:「聽訟,吾猶人也,必也使無訟乎!」
　　子張問政。子曰:「居之無倦,行之以忠。」
　　子曰:「君子博學於文,約之以禮,亦可以弗畔矣夫!」
　　子曰:「君子成人之美,不成人之惡。小人反是。」

齐景公问政于孔子。孔子对曰:「君君,臣臣,父父,子子。」
公曰:「善哉!信如君不君,臣不臣,父不父,子不子,虽有粟,
吾得而食诸?」
　　子曰:「片言可以折狱者,其由也与?」子路无宿诺。
　　子曰:「听讼,吾犹人也,必也使无讼乎!」
　　子张问政。子曰:「居之无倦,行之以忠。」
　　子曰:「君子博学于文,约之以礼,亦可以弗畔矣夫!」
　　子曰:「君子成人之美,不成人之恶。小人反是。」

CHAP. XI. 1. The Duke Ching, of Ch'i, asked Confucius about government. 2. Confucius replied, 'There is government, when the prince is prince, and the minister is minister; when the father is father, and the son is son.' 3. 'Good!' said the duke; 'if, indeed; the prince be not prince, the minister not minister, the father not father, and the son not son, although I have my revenue, can I enjoy it?'

CHAP. XII. 1. The Master said, 'Ah! it is Yu, who could with half a word settle litigations!' 2. Tsze-lu never slept over a promise.

CHAP. XIII. The Master said, 'In hearing litigations, I am like any other body. What is necessary, however, is to cause the people to have no litigations.'

CHAP. XIV. Tsze-chang asked about government. The Master said, 'The art of governing is to keep its affairs before the mind without weariness, and to practise them with undeviating consistency.'

CHAP. XV. The Master said, 'By extensively studying all learning, and keeping himself under the restraint of the rules of propriety, one may thus likewise not err from what is right.'

CHAP. XVI. The Master said, 'The superior man seeks to perfect the admirable qualities of men, and does not seek to perfect their bad qualities. The mean man does the opposite of this.'

SEAL SCRIPT

小
几
凡
是

可
己
弗
即
君
子

君
子
博
學
於
文
約
之
以
禮
亦

君
子
成
人
之
美
不
成
人
之
惡
小
人
反
是

子
張
問
政
子
曰
居
之
無
倦
行
之
以
忠

子
曰
聽
訟
吾
猶
人
也
必
也
使
無
訟
乎

子
曰
片
言
可
以
折
獄
者
其
由
也
與
子
路
無
宿
諾

齊
景
公
問
政
於
孔
子
孔
子
對
曰
君
君
臣
臣
父
父
子
子
公
曰
善
哉
信
如
君

155

　　季康子問政於孔子。孔子對曰：「政者，正也。子帥以正，孰敢不正？」

　　季康子患盜，問於孔子。孔子對曰：「苟子之不欲，雖賞之不竊。」

　　季康子問政於孔子曰：「如殺無道，以就有道，何如？」孔子對曰：「子為政，焉用殺？子欲善，而民善矣。君子之德風，小人之德草。草上之風，必偃。」

SIMPLIFIED CHINESE

　　季康子问政于孔子。孔子对曰：「政者，正也。子帅以正，孰敢不正？」

　　季康子患盜，问于孔子。孔子对曰：「苟子之不欲，虽赏之不窃。」

　　季康子问政于孔子曰：「如杀无道，以就有道，何如？」孔子对曰：「子为政，焉用杀？子欲善，而民善矣。君子之德风，小人之德草。草上之风，必偃。」

CHAP. XVII. Chi K'ang asked Confucius about government. Confucius replied, 'To govern means to rectify. If you lead on the people with correctness, who will dare not to be correct?'

CHAP. XVIII. Chi K'ang, distressed about the number of thieves in the state, inquired of Confucius how to do away with them. Confucius said, 'If you, sir, were not covetous, although you should reward them to do it, they would not steal.'

CHAP. XIX. Chi K'ang asked Confucius about government, saying, 'What do you say to killing the unprincipled for the good of the principled?' Confucius replied, 'Sir, in carrying on your government, why should you use killing at all? Let your evinced desires be for what is good, and the people will be good. The relation between superiors and inferiors, is like that between the wind and the grass. The grass must bend, when the wind blows across it.'

SEAL SCRIPT

　　子張問：「士何如斯可謂之達矣？」子曰：「何哉，爾所謂達者？」子張對曰：「在邦必聞，在家必聞。」子曰：「是聞也，非達也。夫達也者，質直而好義，察言而觀色，慮以下人。在邦必達，在家必達。夫聞也者，色取仁而行違，居之不疑。在邦必聞，在家必聞。」

　　樊遲從遊於舞雩之下，曰：「敢問崇德、脩慝、辨惑。」子曰：「善哉問！先事後得，非崇德與？攻其惡，無攻人之惡，非脩慝與？一朝之忿，忘其身，以及其親，非惑與？」

　　子张问：「士何如斯可谓之达矣？」子曰：「何哉，尔所谓达者？」子张对曰：「在邦必闻，在家必闻。」子曰：「是闻也，非达也。夫达也者，质直而好义，察言而观色，虑以下人。在邦必达，在家必达。夫闻也者，色取仁而行违，居之不疑。在邦必闻，在家必闻。」

　　樊迟从游于舞雩之下，曰：「敢问崇德、修慝、辨惑。」子曰：「善哉问！先事后得，非崇德与？攻其恶，无攻人之恶，非修慝与？一朝之忿，忘其身，以及其亲，非惑与？」

CHAP. XX. 1. Tsze-chang asked, 'What must the officer be, who may be said to be distinguished?' 2. The Master said, 'What is it you call being distinguished?' 3. Tsze-chang replied, 'It is to be heard of through the State, to be heard of throughout his clan.' 4. The Master said, 'That is notoriety, not distinction. 5. 'Now the man of distinction is solid and straightforward, and loves righteousness. He examines people's words, and looks at their countenances. He is anxious to humble himself to others. Such a man will be distinguished in the country; he will be distinguished in his clan. 6. 'As to the man of notoriety, he assumes the appearance of virtue, but his actions are opposed to it, and he rests in this character without any doubts about himself. Such a man will be heard of in the country; he will be heard of in the clan.'

CHAP. XXI. 1. Fan Ch'ih rambling with the Master under the trees about the rain altars, said, 'I venture to ask how to exalt virtue, to correct cherished evil, and to discover delusions.' 2. The Master said, 'Truly a good question! 3. 'If doing what is to be done be made the first business, and success a secondary consideration;— is not this the way to exalt virtue? To assail one's own wickedness and not assail that of others;— is not this the way to correct cherished evil? For a morning's anger to disregard one's own life, and involve that of his parents;— is not this a case of delusion?'

SEAL SCRIPT

　　樊遲問仁。子曰:「愛人。」問知。子曰:「知人。」樊遲未達。子曰:「舉直錯諸枉，能使枉者直。」樊遲退，見子夏。曰:「鄉也吾見於夫子而問知，子曰，『舉直錯諸枉，能使枉者直』，何謂也? 」子夏曰:「富哉言乎! 舜有天下，選於眾，舉皋陶，不仁者遠矣。湯有天下，選於眾，舉伊尹，不仁者遠矣。」

　　子貢問友。子曰:「忠告而善道之，不可則止，無自辱焉。」

　　曾子曰:「君子以文會友，以友輔仁。」

　　樊迟问仁。子曰:「爱人。」问知。子曰:「知人。」樊迟未达。子曰:「举直错诸枉，能使枉者直。」樊迟退，见子夏。曰:「乡也吾见于夫子而问知，子曰，『举直错诸枉，能使枉者直』，何谓也? 」子夏曰:「富哉言乎! 舜有天下，选于众，举皋陶，不仁者远矣。汤有天下，选于众，举伊尹，不仁者远矣。」

　　子贡问友。子曰:「忠告而善道之，不可则止，无自辱焉。」

　　曾子曰:「君子以文会友，以友辅仁。」

CHAP. XXII. 1. Fan Ch'ih asked about benevolence. The Master said, 'It is to love all men.' He asked about knowledge. The Master said, 'It is to know all men.' 2. Fan Ch'ih did not immediately understand these answers. 3. The Master said, 'Employ the upright and put aside all the crooked;— in this way the crooked can be made to be upright.' 4. Fan Ch'ih retired, and, seeing Tsze-hsia, he said to him, 'A Little while ago, I had an interview with our Master, and asked him about knowledge. He said, 'Employ the upright, and put aside all the crooked;— in this way, the crooked will be made to be upright.' What did he mean?' 5. Tsze-hsia said, 'Truly rich is his saying! 6. 'Shun, being in possession of the kingdom, selected from among all the people, and employed Kao-yao, on which all who were devoid of virtue disappeared. T'ang, being in possession of the kingdom, selected from among all the people, and employed I Yin, and all who were devoid of virtue disappeared.'

CHAP. XXIII. Tsze-kung asked about friendship. The Master said, 'Faithfully admonish your friend, and skillfully lead him on. If you find him impracticable, stop. Do not disgrace yourself.'

CHAP. XXIV. The philosopher Tsang said, 'The superior man on grounds of culture meets with his friends, and by their friendship helps his virtue.'

SEAL SCRIPT

161

子路第十三

子路問政。子曰：「先之，勞之。」請益。曰：「無倦。」
仲弓為季氏宰，問政。子曰：「先有司，赦小過，舉賢才。」曰：「焉知賢才而舉之？」曰：「舉爾所知。爾所不知，人其舍諸？」

子路第十三

子路问政。子曰：「先之，劳之。」请益。曰：「无倦。」
仲弓为季氏宰，问政。子曰：「先有司，赦小过，举贤才。」曰：「焉知贤才而举之？」曰：「举尔所知。尔所不知，人其舍诸？」

BOOK XIII. TSZE-LU.

CHAP. I. 1. Tsze-lu asked about government. The Master said, 'Go before the people with your example, and be laborious in their affairs.' 2. He requested further instruction, and was answered, 'Be not weary (in these things).'

CHAP. II. 1. Chung-kung, being chief minister to the Head of the Chi family, asked about government. The Master said, 'Employ first the services of your various officers, pardon small faults, and raise to office men of virtue and talents.' 2. Chung-kung said, 'How shall I know the men of virtue and talent, so that I may raise them to office?' He was answered, 'Raise to office those whom you know. As to those whom you do not know, will others neglect them?'

SEAL SCRIPT

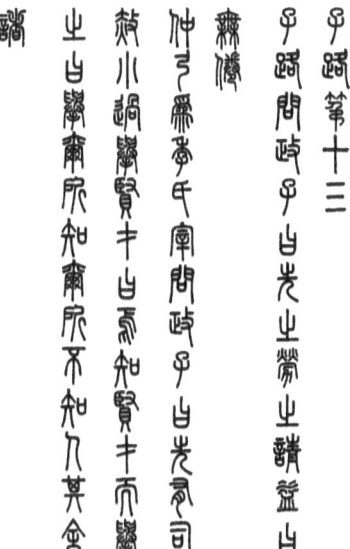

163

子路曰：「衛君待子而為政，子將奚先？」子曰：「必也正名乎！」子路曰：「有是哉，子之迂也！奚其正？」子曰：「野哉由也！君子於其所不知，蓋闕如也。名不正，則言不順；言不順，則事不成；事不成，則禮樂不興；禮樂不興，則刑罰不中；刑罰不中，則民無所措手足。故君子名之必可言也，言之必可行也。君子於其言，無所苟而已矣。」

子路曰：「卫君待子而为政，子将奚先？」子曰：「必也正名乎！」子路曰：「有是哉，子之迂也！奚其正？」子曰：「野哉由也！君子于其所不知，盖阙如也。名不正，则言不顺；言不顺，则事不成；事不成，则礼乐不兴；礼乐不兴，则刑罚不中；刑罚不中，则民无所措手足。故君子名之必可言也，言之必可行也。君子于其言，无所苟而已矣。」

CHAP. III. 1. Tsze-lu said, 'The ruler of Wei has been waiting for you, in order with you to administer the government. What will you consider the first thing to be done?' 2. The Master replied, 'What is necessary is to rectify names.' 3. 'So, indeed!' said Tsze-lu. 'You are wide of the mark! Why must there be such rectification?' 4. The Master said, 'How uncultivated you are, Yu! A superior man, in regard to what he does not know, shows a cautious reserve. 5. 'If names be not correct, language is not in accordance with the truth of things. If language be not in accordance with the truth of things, affairs cannot be carried on to success. 6. 'When affairs cannot be carried on to success, proprieties and music will not flourish. When proprieties and music do not flourish, punishments will not be properly awarded. When punishments are not properly awarded, the people do not know how to move hand or foot. 7. 'Therefore a superior man considers it necessary that the names he uses may be spoken appropriately, and also that what he speaks may be carried out appropriately. What the superior man requires, is just that in his words there may be nothing incorrect.'

SEAL SCRIPT

165

樊遲請學稼，子曰：「吾不如老農。」請學為圃。曰：「吾不如老圃。」樊遲出。子曰：「小人哉，樊須也！上好禮，則民莫敢不敬；上好義，則民莫敢不服；上好信，則民莫敢不用情。夫如是，則四方之民襁負其子而至矣，焉用稼？」

子曰：「誦詩三百，授之以政，不達；使於四方，不能專對；雖多，亦奚以為？」

子曰：「其身正，不令而行；其身不正，雖令不從。」

子曰：「魯衛之政，兄弟也。」

樊迟请学稼，子曰：「吾不如老农。」请学为圃。曰：「吾不如老圃。」樊迟出。子曰：「小人哉，樊须也！上好礼，则民莫敢不敬；上好义，则民莫敢不服；上好信，则民莫敢不用情。夫如是，则四方之民襁负其子而至矣，焉用稼？」

子曰：「诵诗三百，授之以政，不达；使于四方，不能专对；虽多，亦奚以为？」

子曰：「其身正，不令而行；其身不正，虽令不从。」

子曰：「鲁卫之政，兄弟也。」

CHAP. IV. 1. Fan Ch'ih requested to be taught husbandry. The Master said, 'I am not so good for that as an old husbandman.' He requested also to be taught gardening, and was answered, 'I am not so good for that as an old gardener.' 2. Fan Ch'ih having gone out, the Master said, 'A small man, indeed, is Fan Hsu! 3. If a superior love propriety, the people will not dare not to be reverent. If he love righteousness, the people will not dare not to submit to his example. If he love good faith, the people will not dare not to be sincere. Now, when these things obtain, the people from all quarters will come to him, bearing their children on their backs;— what need has he of a knowledge of husbandry?'

CHAP. V. The Master said, 'Though a man may be able to recite the three hundred odes, yet if, when intrusted with a governmental charge, he knows not how to act, or if, when sent to any quarter on a mission, he cannot give his replies unassisted, notwithstanding the extent of his learning, of what practical use is it?'

CHAP. VI. The Master said, 'When a prince's personal conduct is correct, his government is effective without the issuing of orders. If his personal conduct is not correct, he may issue orders, but they will not be followed.'

CHAP. VII. The Master said, 'The governments of Lu and Wei are brothers.'

SEAL SCRIPT

167

　　子謂衛公子荊，「善居室。始有，曰：『苟合矣。』少有，曰：『苟完矣。』富有，曰：『苟美矣。』」

　　子適衛，冉有僕。子曰：「庶矣哉！」冉有曰：「既庶矣。又何加焉？」曰：「富之。」曰：「既富矣，又何加焉？」曰：「教之。」

　　子曰：「苟有用我者。期月而已可也，三年有成。」

　　子曰：「善人為邦百年，亦可以勝殘去殺矣。誠哉是言也！」

　　子曰：「如有王者，必世而後仁。」

　　子谓卫公子荆，「善居室。始有，曰：『苟合矣。』少有，曰：『苟完矣。』富有，曰：『苟美矣。』」

　　子适卫，冉有仆。子曰：「庶矣哉！」冉有曰：「既庶矣。又何加焉？」曰：「富之。」曰：「既富矣，又何加焉？」曰：「教之。」

　　子曰：「苟有用我者。期月而已可也，三年有成。」

　　子曰：「善人为邦百年，亦可以胜残去杀矣。诚哉是言也！」

　　子曰：「如有王者，必世而后仁。」

CHAP. VIII. The Master said of Ching, a scion of the ducal family of Wei, that he knew the economy of a family well. When he began to have means, he said, 'Ha! here is a collection!' When they were a little increased, he said, 'Ha! this is complete!' When he had become rich, he said, 'Ha! this is admirable!'

CHAP. IX. 1. When the Master went to Wei, Zan Yu acted as driver of his carriage. 2. The Master observed, 'How numerous are the people!' 3. Yu said, 'Since they are thus numerous, what more shall be done for them?' 'Enrich them,' was the reply. 4. 'And when they have been enriched, what more shall be done?' The Master said, 'Teach them.'

CHAP. X. The Master said, 'If there were (any of the princes) who would employ me, in the course of twelve months, I should have done something considerable. In three years, the government would be perfected.'

CHAP. XI. The Master said, '"If good men were to govern a country in succession for a hundred years, they would be able to transform the violently bad, and dispense with capital punishments." True indeed is this saying!'

CHAP. XII. The Master said, 'If a truly royal ruler were to arise, it would still require a generation, and then virtue would prevail.'

SEAL SCRIPT

子謂衛公子荊善居室始有曰苟合矣少有曰苟完矣富有曰苟美矣

子適衛冉有僕子曰庶矣哉冉有曰既庶矣又何加焉曰富之曰既富矣又何加焉曰教之

子曰苟有用我者期月而已可也三年有成

子曰善人為邦百年亦可以勝殘去殺矣誠哉是言也

子曰如有王者必世而後仁

子曰：「苟正其身矣，於從政乎何有？不能正其身，如正人何？」

冉子退朝。子曰：「何晏也？」對曰：「有政。」子曰：「其事也。如有政，雖不吾以，吾其與聞之。」

定公問：「一言而可以興邦，有諸？」孔子對曰：「言不可以若是其幾也。人之言曰：『為君難，為臣不易。』如知為君之難也，不幾乎一言而興邦乎？」曰：「一言而喪邦，有諸？」孔子對曰：「言不可以若是其幾也。人之言曰：『予無樂乎為君，唯其言而莫予違也。』如其善而莫之違也，不亦善乎？如不善而莫之違也，不幾乎一言而喪邦乎？」

子曰：「苟正其身矣，于从政乎何有？不能正其身，如正人何？」

冉子退朝。子曰：「何晏也？」对曰：「有政。」子曰：「其事也。如有政，虽不吾以，吾其与闻之。」

定公问：「一言而可以兴邦，有诸？」孔子对曰：「言不可以若是其几也。人之言曰：『为君难，为臣不易。』如知为君之难也，不几乎一言而兴邦乎？」曰：「一言而丧邦，有诸？」孔子对曰：「言不可以若是其几也。人之言曰：『予无乐乎为君，唯其言而莫予违也。』如其善而莫之违也，不亦善乎？如不善而莫之违也，不几乎一言而丧邦乎？」

CHAP. XIII. The Master said, 'If a minister make his own conduct correct, what difficulty will he have in assisting in government? If he cannot rectify himself, what has he to do with rectifying others?'

CHAP. XIV. The disciple Zan returning from the court, the Master said to him, 'How are you so late?' He replied, 'We had government business.' The Master said, 'It must have been family affairs. If there had been government business, though I am not now in office, I should have been consulted about it.'

CHAP. XV. 1. The Duke Ting asked whether there was a single sentence which could make a country prosperous. Confucius replied, 'Such an effect cannot be expected from one sentence. 2. 'There is a saying, however, which people have— "To be a prince is difficult; to be a minister is not easy." 3. 'If a ruler knows this,— the difficulty of being a prince,— may there not be expected from this one sentence the prosperity of his country?' 4. The duke then said, 'Is there a single sentence which can ruin a country?' Confucius replied, 'Such an effect as that cannot be expected from one sentence. There is, however, the saying which people have— "I have no pleasure in being a prince, but only in that no one can offer any opposition to what I say!" 5. 'If a ruler's words be good, is it not also good that no one oppose them? But if they are not good, and no one opposes them, may there not be expected from this one sentence the ruin of his country?'

葉公問政。子曰：「近者說，遠者來。」

子夏為莒父宰，問政。子曰：「無欲速，無見小利。欲速，則不達；見小利，則大事不成。」

葉公語孔子曰：「吾黨有直躬者，其父攘羊，而子證之。」孔子曰：「吾黨之直者異於是。父為子隱，子為父隱，直在其中矣。」

樊遲問仁。子曰：「居處恭，執事敬，與人忠。雖之夷狄，不可棄也。」

叶公问政。子曰：「近者说，远者来。」

子夏为莒父宰，问政。子曰：「无欲速，无见小利。欲速，则不达；见小利，则大事不成。」

叶公语孔子曰：「吾党有直躬者，其父攘羊，而子证之。」孔子曰：「吾党之直者异于是。父为子隐，子为父隐，直在其中矣。」

樊迟问仁。子曰：「居处恭，执事敬，与人忠。虽之夷狄，不可弃也。」

CHAP. XVI. 1. The Duke of Sheh asked about government. 2. The Master said, 'Good government obtains, when those who are near are made happy, and those who are far off are attracted.'

CHAP. XVII. Tsze-hsia, being governor of Chu-fu, asked about government. The Master said, 'Do not be desirous to have things done quickly; do not look at small advantages. Desire to have things done quickly prevents their being done thoroughly. Looking at small advantages prevents great affairs from being accomplished.'

CHAP. XVIII. 1. The Duke of Sheh informed Confucius, saying, 'Among us here there are those who may be styled upright in their conduct. If their father have stolen a sheep, they will bear witness to the fact.' 2. Confucius said, 'Among us, in our part of the country, those who are upright are different from this. The father conceals the misconduct of the son, and the son conceals the misconduct of the father. Uprightness is to be found in this.'

CHAP. XIX. Fan Ch'ih asked about perfect virtue. The Master said, 'It is, in retirement, to be sedately grave; in the management of business, to be reverently attentive; in intercourse with others, to be strictly sincere. Though a man go among rude, uncultivated tribes, these qualities may not be neglected.'

SEAL SCRIPT

子貢問曰：「何如斯可謂之士矣？」子曰：「行己有恥，使
於四方，不辱君命，可謂士矣。」曰：「敢問其次。」曰：「宗族
稱孝焉，鄉黨稱弟焉。」曰：「敢問其次。」曰：「言必信，行必
果，硜硜然小人哉！抑亦可以為次矣。」曰：「今之從政者何如？」
子曰：「噫！斗筲之人，何足算也。」

子曰：「不得中行而與之，必也狂狷乎！狂者進取，狷者有
所不為也。」

子贡问曰：「何如斯可谓之士矣？」子曰：「行己有耻，使
于四方，不辱君命，可谓士矣。」曰：「敢问其次。」曰：「宗族
称孝焉，乡党称弟焉。」曰：「敢问其次。」曰：「言必信，行必
果，硁硁然小人哉！抑亦可以为次矣。」曰：「今之从政者何如？」
子曰：「噫！斗筲之人，何足算也。」

子曰：「不得中行而与之，必也狂狷乎！狂者进取，狷者有
所不为也。」

CHAP. XX. 1. Tsze-kung asked, saying, 'What qualities must a man possess to entitle him to be called an officer? The Master said, 'He who in his conduct of himself maintains a sense of shame, and when sent to any quarter will not disgrace his prince's commission, deserves to be called an officer.' 3. Tsze-kung pursued, 'I venture to ask who may be placed in the next lower rank?' And he was told, 'He whom the circle of his relatives pronounce to be filial, whom his fellow-villagers and neighbours pronounce to be fraternal.' 3. Again the disciple asked, 'I venture to ask about the class still next in order.' The Master said, 'They are determined to be sincere in what they say, and to carry out what they do. They are obstinate little men. Yet perhaps they may make the next class.' 4. Tsze-kung finally inquired, 'Of what sort are those of the present day, who engage in government?' The Master said 'Pooh! they are so many pecks and hampers, not worth being taken into account.'

CHAP. XXI. The Master said, 'Since I cannot get men pursuing the due medium, to whom I might communicate my instructions, I must find the ardent and the cautiously-decided. The ardent will advance and lay hold of truth; the cautiously-decided will keep themselves from what is wrong.'

SEAL SCRIPT

　　子曰：「南人有言曰：『人而無恆，不可以作巫醫。』善夫！」「不恆其德，或承之羞。」子曰：「不占而已矣。」

　　子曰：「君子和而不同，小人同而不和。」

　　子貢問曰：「鄉人皆好之，何如？」子曰：「未可也。」「鄉人皆惡之，何如？」子曰：「未可也。不如鄉人之善者好之，其不善者惡之。」

　　子曰：「南人有言曰：『人而无恒，不可以作巫医。』善夫！」「不恒其德，或承之羞。」子曰：「不占而已矣。」

　　子曰：「君子和而不同，小人同而不和。」

　　子贡问曰：「乡人皆好之，何如？」子曰：「未可也。」「乡人皆恶之，何如？」子曰：「未可也。不如乡人之善者好之，其不善者恶之。」

CHAP. XXII. 1. The Master said, 'The people of the south have a saying— "A man without constancy cannot be either a wizard or a doctor." Good! 2. 'Inconstant in his virtue, he will be visited with disgrace.' 3. The Master said, 'This arises simply from not attending to the prognostication.'

CHAP. XXIII. The Master said, 'The superior man is affable, but not adulatory; the mean man is adulatory, but not affable.'

CHAP. XXIV. Tsze-kung asked, saying, 'What do you say of a man who is loved by all the people of his neighborhood?' The Master replied, 'We may not for that accord our approval of him.' 'And what do you say of him who is hated by all the people of his neighborhood?' The Master said, 'We may not for that conclude that he is bad. It is better than either of these cases that the good in the neighborhood love him, and the bad hate him.'

SEAL SCRIPT

　　子曰：「君子易事而難說也：說之不以道，不說也；及其使人也，器之。小人難事而易說也：說之雖不以道，說也；及其使人也，求備焉。」

　　子曰：「君子泰而不驕，小人驕而不泰。」

　　子曰：「剛毅、木訥，近仁。」

　　子路問曰：「何如斯可謂之士矣？」子曰：「切切、偲偲、怡怡如也，可謂士矣。朋友切切、偲偲，兄弟怡怡。」

　　子曰：「善人教民七年，亦可以即戎矣。」

　　子曰：「以不教民戰，是謂棄之。」

　　子曰：「君子易事而难说也：说之不以道，不说也；及其使人也，器之。小人难事而易说也：说之虽不以道，说也；及其使人也，求备焉。」

　　子曰：「君子泰而不骄，小人骄而不泰。」

　　子曰：「刚毅、木讷，近仁。」

　　子路问曰：「何如斯可谓之士矣？」子曰：「切切、偲偲、怡怡如也，可谓士矣。朋友切切、偲偲，兄弟怡怡。」

　　子曰：「善人教民七年，亦可以即戎矣。」

　　子曰：「以不教民战，是谓弃之。」

CHAP. XXV. The Master said, 'The superior man is easy to serve and difficult to please. If you try to please him in any way which is not accordant with right, he will not be pleased. But in his employment of men, he uses them according to their capacity. The mean man is difficult to serve, and easy to please. If you try to please him, though it be in a way which is not accordant with right, he may be pleased. But in his employment of men, he wishes them to be equal to everything.'

CHAP. XXVI. The Master said, 'The superior man has a dignified ease without pride. The mean man has pride without a dignified ease.'

CHAP. XXVII. The Master said, 'The firm, the enduring, the simple, and the modest are near to virtue.'

CHAP. XXVIII. Tsze-lu asked, saying, 'What qualities must a man possess to entitle him to be called a scholar?' The Master said, 'He must be thus,—earnest, urgent, and bland:— among his friends, earnest and urgent; among his brethren, bland.'

CHAP. XXIX. The Master said, 'Let a good man teach the people seven years, and they may then likewise be employed in war.'

CHAP. XXX. The Master said, 'To lead an uninstructed people to war, is to throw them away.'

SEAL SCRIPT

憲問第十四

　　憲問恥。子曰：「邦有道，穀；邦無道，穀，恥也。」「克、伐、怨、欲不行焉，可以為仁矣？」子曰：「可以為難矣，仁則吾不知也。」

　　子曰：「士而懷居，不足以為士矣。」

　　子曰：「邦有道，危言危行；邦無道，危行言孫。」

　　子曰：「有德者，必有言。有言者，不必有德。仁者，必有勇。勇者，不必有仁。」

宪问第十四

　　宪问耻。子曰：「邦有道，谷；邦无道，谷，耻也。」「克、伐、怨、欲不行焉，可以为仁矣？」子曰：「可以为难矣，仁则吾不知也。」

　　子曰：「士而怀居，不足以为士矣。」

　　子曰：「邦有道，危言危行；邦无道，危行言孙。」

　　子曰：「有德者，必有言。有言者，不必有德。仁者，必有勇。勇者，不必有仁。」

BOOK XIV. HSIEN WAN.

CHAP. I. Hsien asked what was shameful. The Master said, 'When good government prevails in a state, to be thinking only of salary; and, when bad government prevails, to be thinking, in the same way, only of salary;— this is shameful.'

CHAP. II. 1. 'When the love of superiority, boasting, resentments, and covetousness are repressed, this may be deemed perfect virtue.' 2. The Master said, 'This may be regarded as the achievement of what is difficult. But I do not know that it is to be deemed perfect virtue.'

CHAP. III. The Master said, 'The scholar who cherishes the love of comfort is not fit to be deemed a scholar.'

CHAP. IV. The Master said, 'When good government prevails in a state, language may be lofty and bold, and actions the same. When bad government prevails, the actions may be lofty and bold, but the language may be with some reserve.'

CHAP. V. The Master said, 'The virtuous will be sure to speak correctly, but those whose speech is good may not always be virtuous. Men of principle are sure to be bold, but those who are bold may not always be men of principle.'

SEAL SCRIPT

　　南宮适問於孔子曰：「羿善射，奡盪舟，俱不得其死然；禹稷躬稼，而有天下。」夫子不答，南宮适出。子曰：「君子哉若人！尚德哉若人！」

　　子曰：「君子而不仁者有矣夫，未有小人而仁者也。」

　　子曰：「愛之，能勿勞乎？忠焉，能勿誨乎？」

　　子曰：「為命：裨諶草創之，世叔討論之，行人子羽脩飾之，東里子產潤色之。」

　　南宫适问于孔子曰：「羿善射，奡荡舟，俱不得其死然；禹稷躬稼，而有天下。」夫子不答，南宫适出。子曰：「君子哉若人！尚德哉若人！」

　　子曰：「君子而不仁者有矣夫，未有小人而仁者也。」

　　子曰：「爱之，能勿劳乎？忠焉，能勿诲乎？」

　　子曰：「为命：裨谌草创之，世叔讨论之，行人子羽修饰之，东里子产润色之。」

CHAP. VI. Nan-kung Kwo, submitting an inquiry to Confucius, said, 'I was skillful at archery, and Ao could move a boat along upon the land, but neither of them died a natural death. Yu and Chi personally wrought at the toils of husbandry, and they became possessors of the kingdom.' The Master made no reply; but when Nan-kung Kwo went out, he said, 'A superior man indeed is this! An esteemer of virtue indeed is this!'

CHAP. VII. The Master said, 'Superior men, and yet not always virtuous, there have been, alas! But there never has been a mean man, and, at the same time, virtuous.'

CHAP. VIII. The Master said, 'Can there be love which does not lead to strictness with its object? Can there be loyalty which does not lead to the instruction of its object?'

CHAP. IX. The Master said, 'In preparing the governmental notifications, P'i Shan first made the rough draft; Shi-shu examined and discussed its contents; Tsze-yu, the manager of Foreign intercourse, then polished the style; and, finally, Tsze-ch'an of Tung-li gave it the proper elegance and finish.'

SEAL SCRIPT

183

　　或問子產。子曰：「惠人也。」問子西。曰：「彼哉！彼哉！」
問管仲。曰：「人也。奪伯氏駢邑三百，飯疏食，沒齒，無怨言。」
　　子曰：「貧而無怨難，富而無驕易。」
　　子曰：「孟公綽，為趙魏老則優，不可以為滕薛大夫。」
　　子路問成人。子曰：「若臧武仲之知，公綽之不欲，卞莊子
之勇，冉求之藝，文之以禮樂，亦可以為成人矣。」曰：「今之
成人者何必然？見利思義，見危授命，久要不忘平生之言，亦
可以為成人矣。」

　　或问子产。子曰：「惠人也。」问子西。曰：「彼哉！彼哉！」
问管仲。曰：「人也。夺伯氏骈邑三百，饭疏食，没齿，无怨言。」
　　子曰：「贫而无怨难，富而无骄易。」
　　子曰：「孟公绰，为赵魏老则优，不可以为滕薛大夫。」
　　子路问成人。子曰：「若臧武仲之知，公绰之不欲，卞庄子
之勇，冉求之艺，文之以礼乐，亦可以为成人矣。」曰：「今之
成人者何必然？见利思义，见危授命，久要不忘平生之言，亦
可以为成人矣。」

CHAP. X. 1. Some one asked about Tsze-ch'an. The Master said, 'He was a kind man.' 2. He asked about Tsze-hsi. The Master said, 'That man! That man!' 3. He asked about Kwan Chung. 'For him,' said the Master, 'the city of Pien, with three hundred families, was taken from the chief of the Po family, who did not utter a murmuring word, though, to the end of his life, he had only coarse rice to eat.'

CHAP. XI. The Master said, 'To be poor without murmuring is difficult. To be rich without being proud is easy.'

CHAP. XII. The Master said, 'Mang Kung-ch'o is more than fit to be chief officer in the families of Chao and Wei, but he is not fit to be great officer to either of the States Tang or Hsieh.'

CHAP. XIII. 1. Tsze-lu asked what constituted a COMPLETE man. The Master said, 'Suppose a man with the knowledge of Tsang Wu-chung, the freedom from covetousness of Kung-ch'o, the bravery of Chwang of Pien, and the varied talents of Zan Ch'iu; add to these the accomplishments of the rules of propriety and music:— such a one might be reckoned a COMPLETE man.' 2. He then added, 'But what is the necessity for a complete man of the present day to have all these things? The man, who in the view of gain, thinks of righteousness; who in the view of danger is prepared to give up his life; and who does not forget an old agreement however far back it extends:— such a man may be reckoned a COMPLETE man.'

SEAL SCRIPT

185

　　子問公叔文子於公明賈曰：「信乎夫子不言、不笑、不取乎？」公明賈對曰：「以告者過也。夫子時然後言，人不厭其言；樂然後笑，人不厭其笑；義然後取，人不厭其取。」子曰：「其然，豈其然乎？」

　　子曰：「臧武仲以防求為後於魯，雖曰不要君，吾不信也。」

　　子曰：「晉文公譎而不正，齊桓公正而不譎。」

　　子路曰：「桓公殺公子糾，召忽死之，管仲不死。」曰：「未仁乎？」子曰：「桓公九合諸侯，不以兵車，管仲之力也。如其仁！如其仁！」

SIMPLIFIED CHINESE

　　子问公叔文子于公明贾曰：「信乎夫子不言、不笑、不取乎？」公明贾对曰：「以告者过也。夫子时然后言，人不厌其言；乐然后笑，人不厌其笑；义然后取，人不厌其取。」子曰：「其然，岂其然乎？」

　　子曰：「臧武仲以防求为后于鲁，虽曰不要君，吾不信也。」

　　子曰：「晋文公谲而不正，齐桓公正而不谲。」

　　子路曰：「桓公杀公子纠，召忽死之，管仲不死。」曰：「未仁乎？」子曰：「桓公九合诸侯，不以兵车，管仲之力也。如其仁！如其仁！」

CHAP. XIV. 1. The Master asked Kung-ming Chia about Kung- shu Wan, saying, 'Is it true that your master speaks not, laughs not, and takes not?' 2. Kung-ming Chia replied, 'This has arisen from the reporters going beyond the truth.— My master speaks when it is the time to speak, and so men do not get tired of his speaking. He laughs when there is occasion to be joyful, and so men do not get tired of his laughing. He takes when it is consistent with righteousness to do so, and so men do not get tired of his taking.' The Master said, 'So! But is it so with him?'

CHAP. XV. The Master said, 'Tsang Wu-chung, keeping possession of Fang, asked of the duke of Lu to appoint a successor to him in his family. Although it may be said that he was not using force with his sovereign, I believe he was.'

CHAP. XVI. The Master said, 'The duke Wan of Tsin was crafty and not upright. The duke Hwan of Ch'i was upright and not crafty.'

CHAP. XVII. 1. Tsze-lu said, 'The Duke Hwan caused his brother Chiu to be killed, when Shao Hu died with his master, but Kwan Chung did not die. May not I say that he was wanting in virtue?' 2. The Master said, 'The Duke Hwan assembled all the princes together, and that not with weapons of war and chariots:— it was all through the influence of Kwan Chung. Whose beneficence was like his? Whose beneficence was like his?'

SEAL SCRIPT

子貢曰:「管仲非仁者與?桓公殺公子糾,不能死,又相之。」子曰:「管仲相桓公,霸諸侯,一匡天下,民到于今受其賜。微管仲,吾其被髮左衽矣。豈若匹夫匹婦之為諒也,自經於溝瀆,而莫之知也。」

公叔文子之臣大夫僎,與文子同升諸公。子聞之曰:「可以為文矣。」

子贡曰:「管仲非仁者与?桓公杀公子纠,不能死,又相之。」子曰:「管仲相桓公,霸诸侯,一匡天下,民到于今受其赐。微管仲,吾其被发左衽矣。岂若匹夫匹妇之为谅也,自经于沟渎,而莫之知也。」

公叔文子之臣大夫僎,与文子同升诸公。子闻之曰:「可以为文矣。」

CHAP. XVIII. 1. Tsze-kung said, 'Kwan Chung, I apprehend, was wanting in virtue. When the Duke Hwan caused his brother Chiu to be killed, Kwan Chung was not able to die with him. Moreover, he became prime minister to Hwan.' 2. The Master said, 'Kwan Chung acted as prime minister to the Duke Hwan, made him leader of all the princes, and united and rectified the whole kingdom. Down to the present day, the people enjoy the gifts which he conferred. But for Kwan Chung, we should now be wearing our hair unbound, and the lappets of our coats buttoning on the left side. 3. 'Will you require from him the small fidelity of common men and common women, who would commit suicide in a stream or ditch, no one knowing anything about them?'

CHAP. XIX. 1. The great officer, Hsien, who had been family- minister to Kung-shu Wan, ascended to the prince's court in company with Wan. 2. The Master, having heard of it, said, 'He deserved to be considered WAN (the accomplished).'

SEAL SCRIPT

　　子言衛靈公之無道也，康子曰：「夫如是，奚而不喪？」孔子曰：「仲叔圉治賓客，祝鮀治宗廟，王孫賈治軍旅。夫如是，奚其喪？」

　　子曰：「其言之不怍，則為之也難。」

　　陳成子弒簡公。孔子沐浴而朝，告於哀公曰：「陳恆弒其君，請討之。」公曰：「告夫三子！」孔子曰：「以吾從大夫之後，不敢不告也。君曰『告夫三子』者。」之三子告，不可。孔子曰：「以吾從大夫之後，不敢不告也。」

　　子路問事君。子曰：「勿欺也，而犯之。」

　　子言卫灵公之无道也，康子曰：「夫如是，奚而不丧？」孔子曰：「仲叔圉治宾客，祝鮀治宗庙，王孙贾治军旅。夫如是，奚其丧？」

　　子曰：「其言之不怍，则为之也难。」

　　陈成子弒简公。孔子沐浴而朝，告于哀公曰：「陈恒弒其君，请讨之。」公曰：「告夫三子！」孔子曰：「以吾从大夫之后，不敢不告也。君曰『告夫三子』者。」之三子告，不可。孔子曰：「以吾从大夫之后，不敢不告也。」

　　子路问事君。子曰：「勿欺也，而犯之。」

CHAP. XX. 1. The Master was speaking about the unprincipled course of the duke Ling of Wei, when Ch'i K'ang said, 'Since he is of such a character, how is it he does not lose his State?' 2. Confucius said, 'The Chung-shu Yu has the superintendence of his guests and of strangers; the litanist, T'o, has the management of his ancestral temple; and Wang-sun Chia has the direction of the army and forces:— with such officers as these, how should he lose his State?'

CHAP. XXI. The Master said, 'He who speaks without modesty will find it difficult to make his words good.'

CHAP. XXII. 1. Chan Ch'ang murdered the Duke Chien of Ch'i. 2. Confucius bathed, went to court, and informed the duke Ai, saying, 'Chan Hang has slain his sovereign. I beg that you will undertake to punish him.' 3. The duke said, 'Inform the chiefs of the three families of it.' 4. Confucius retired, and said, 'Following in the rear of the great officers, I did not dare not to represent such a matter, and my prince says, "Inform the chiefs of the three families of it."' 5. He went to the chiefs, and informed them, but they would not act. Confucius then said, 'Following in the rear of the great officers, I did not dare not to represent such a matter.'

CHAP. XXIII. Tsze-lu asked how a ruler should be served. The Master said, 'Do not impose on him, and, moreover, withstand him to his face.'

SEAL SCRIPT

子曰：「君子上達，小人下達。」

子曰：「古之學者為己，今之學者為人。」

蘧伯玉使人於孔子。孔子與之坐而問焉，曰：「夫子何為？」對曰：「夫子欲寡其過而未能也。」使者出。子曰：「使乎！使乎！」

子曰：「不在其位，不謀其政。」曾子曰：「君子思不出其位。」

子曰：「君子恥其言而過其行。」

子曰：「君子道者三，我無能焉：仁者不憂，知者不惑，勇者不懼。」子貢曰：「夫子自道也。」

子曰：「君子上达，小人下达。」

子曰：「古之学者为己，今之学者为人。」

蘧伯玉使人于孔子。孔子与之坐而问焉，曰：「夫子何为？」对曰：「夫子欲寡其过而未能也。」使者出。子曰：「使乎！使乎！」

子曰：「不在其位，不谋其政。」曾子曰：「君子思不出其位。」

子曰：「君子耻其言而过其行。」

子曰：「君子道者三，我无能焉：仁者不忧，知者不惑，勇者不惧。」子贡曰：「夫子自道也。」

CHAP. XXIV. The Master said, 'The progress of the superior man is upwards; the progress of the mean man is downwards.'

CHAP. XXV. The Master said, 'In ancient times, men learned with a view to their own improvement. Now-a-days, men learn with a view to the approbation of others.'

CHAP. XXVI. 1. Chu Po-yu sent a messenger with friendly inquiries to Confucius. 2. Confucius sat with him, and questioned him. 'What,' said he, 'is your master engaged in?' The messenger replied, 'My master is anxious to make his faults few, but he has not yet succeeded.' He then went out, and the Master said, 'A messenger indeed! A messenger indeed!'

CHAP. XXVII. The Master said, 'He who is not in any particular office, has nothing to do with plans for the administration of its duties.'

CHAP. XXVIII. The philosopher Tsang said, 'The superior man, in his thoughts, does not go out of his place.'

CHAP. XXIX. The Master said, 'The superior man is modest in his speech, but exceeds in his actions.'

CHAP. XXX. 1. The Master said, 'The way of the superior man is threefold, but I am not equal to it. Virtuous, he is free from anxieties; wise, he is free from perplexities; bold, he is free from fear. 2. Tsze-kung said, 'Master, that is what you yourself say.'

SEAL SCRIPT

子貢方人。子曰：「賜也賢乎哉？夫我則不暇。」

子曰：「不患人之不己知，患其不能也。」

子曰：「不逆詐，不億不信。抑亦先覺者，是賢乎！」

微生畝謂孔子曰：「丘何為是栖栖者與？無乃為佞乎？」孔子曰：「非敢為佞也，疾固也。」

子曰：「驥不稱其力，稱其德也。」

或曰：「以德報怨，何如？」子曰：「何以報德？以直報怨，以德報德。」

子贡方人。子曰：「赐也贤乎哉？夫我则不暇。」

子曰：「不患人之不己知，患其不能也。」

子曰：「不逆诈，不亿不信。抑亦先觉者，是贤乎！」

微生亩谓孔子曰：「丘何为是栖栖者与？无乃为佞乎？」孔子曰：「非敢为佞也，疾固也。」

子曰：「骥不称其力，称其德也。」

或曰：「以德报怨，何如？」子曰：「何以报德？以直报怨，以德报德。」

CHAP. XXXI. Tsze-kung was in the habit of comparing men together. The Master said, 'Tsze must have reached a high pitch of excellence! Now, I have not leisure for this.'

CHAP. XXXII. The Master said, 'I will not be concerned at men's not knowing me; I will be concerned at my own want of ability.'

CHAP. XXXIII. The Master said, 'He who does not anticipate attempts to deceive him, nor think beforehand of his not being believed, and yet apprehends these things readily (when they occur);— is he not a man of superior worth?'

CHAP. XXXIV. 1. Wei-shang Mau said to Confucius, 'Ch'iu, how is it that you keep roosting about? Is it not that you are an insinuating talker?' 2. Confucius said, 'I do not dare to play the part of such a talker, but I hate obstinacy.'

CHAP. XXXV. The Master said, 'A horse is called a ch'i, not because of its strength, but because of its other good qualities.'

CHAP. XXXVI. 1. Some one said, 'What do you say concerning the principle that injury should be recompensed with kindness?' 2. The Master said, 'With what then will you recompense kindness? 3. 'Recompense injury with justice, and recompense kindness with kindness.'

SEAL SCRIPT

　　子曰：「莫我知也夫！」子貢曰：「何為其莫知子也？」子曰：「不怨天，不尤人。下學而上達。知我者，其天乎！」

　　公伯寮愬子路於季孫。子服景伯以告，曰：「夫子固有惑志於公伯寮，吾力猶能肆諸市朝。」子曰：「道之將行也與？命也。道之將廢也與？命也。公伯寮其如命何！」

　　子曰：「賢者辟世，其次辟地，其次辟色，其次辟言。」子曰：「作者七人矣。」

　　子曰：「莫我知也夫！」子贡曰：「何为其莫知子也？」子曰：「不怨天，不尤人。下学而上达。知我者，其天乎！」

　　公伯寮愬子路于季孙。子服景伯以告，曰：「夫子固有惑志于公伯寮，吾力犹能肆诸市朝。」子曰：「道之将行也与？命也。道之将废也与？命也。公伯寮其如命何！」

　　子曰：「贤者辟世，其次辟地，其次辟色，其次辟言。」子曰：「作者七人矣。」

CHAP. XXXVII. 1. The Master said, 'Alas! there is no one that knows me.' 2. Tsze-kung said, 'What do you mean by thus saying— that no one knows you?' The Master replied, 'I do not murmur against Heaven. I do not grumble against men. My studies lie low, and my penetration rises high. But there is Heaven;— that knows me!'

CHAP. XXXVIII. 1. The Kung-po Liao, having slandered Tsze-lu to Chi-sun, Tsze-fu Ching-po informed Confucius of it, saying, 'Our master is certainly being led astray by the Kung-po Liao, but I have still power enough left to cut Liao off, and expose his corpse in the market and in the court.' 2. The Master said, 'If my principles are to advance, it is so ordered. If they are to fall to the ground, it is so ordered. What can the Kung-po Liao do where such ordering is concerned?'

CHAP. XXXIX. 1. The Master said, 'Some men of worth retire from the world. 2. Some retire from particular states. 3. Some retire because of disrespect-ful looks. 4. Some retire because of contradictory language.'

CHAP. XL. The Master said, 'Those who have done this are seven men.'

SEAL SCRIPT

197

　　子路宿於石門。晨門曰：「奚自？」子路曰：「自孔氏。」曰：「是知其不可而為之者與？」

　　子擊磬於衛。有荷蕢而過孔氏之門者，曰：「有心哉！擊磬乎！」既而曰：「鄙哉！硜硜乎！莫己知也，斯己而已矣。深則厲，淺則揭。」子曰：「果哉！末之難矣。」

　　子張曰：「《書》云：『高宗諒陰，三年不言。』何謂也？」子曰：「何必高宗，古之人皆然。君薨，百官總己以聽於冢宰，三年。」

　　子路宿于石门。晨门曰：「奚自？」子路曰：「自孔氏。」曰：「是知其不可而为之者与？」

　　子击磬于卫。有荷蒉而过孔氏之门者，曰：「有心哉！击磬乎！」既而曰：「鄙哉！硁硁乎！莫己知也，斯己而已矣。深则厉，浅则揭。」子曰：「果哉！末之难矣。」

　　子张曰：「《书》云：『高宗谅阴，三年不言。』何谓也？」子曰：「何必高宗，古之人皆然。君薨，百官总己以听于冢宰，三年。」

CHAP. XLI. Tsze-lu happening to pass the night in Shih-man, the gatekeeper said to him, 'Whom do you come from?' Tsze-lu said, 'From Mr. K'ung.' 'It is he,— is it not?'— said the other, 'who knows the impracticable nature of the times and yet will be doing in them.'

CHAP. XLII. 1. The Master was playing, one day, on a musical stone in Wei, when a man, carrying a straw basket, passed the door of the house where Confucius was, and said, 'His heart is full who so beats the musical stone.' 2. A little while after, he added, 'How contemptible is the one-ideaed obstinacy those sounds display! When one is taken no notice of, he has simply at once to give over his wish for public employment. "Deep water must be crossed with the clothes on; shallow water may be crossed with the clothes held up."' 3. The Master said, 'How determined is he in his purpose! But this is not difficult!'

CHAP. XLIII. 1. Tsze-chang said, 'What is meant when the Shu says that Kao-tsung, while observing the usual imperial mourning, was for three years without speaking?' 2. The Master said, 'Why must Kao-tsung be referred to as an example of this? The ancients all did so. When the sovereign died, the officers all attended to their several duties, taking instructions from the prime minister for three years.'

SEAL SCRIPT

子曰：「上好禮，則民易使也。」

子路問君子。子曰：「脩己以敬。」曰：「如斯而已乎？」曰：「脩己以安人。」曰：「如斯而已乎？」曰：「脩己以安百姓。脩己以安百姓，堯舜其猶病諸！」

原壤夷俟。子曰：「幼而不孫弟，長而無述焉，老而不死，是為賊！」以杖叩其脛。

闕黨童子將命。或問之曰：「益者與？」子曰：「吾見其居於位也，見其與先生並行也。非求益者也，欲速成者也。」

子曰：「上好礼，则民易使也。」

子路问君子。子曰：「修己以敬。」曰：「如斯而已乎？」曰：「修己以安人。」曰：「如斯而已乎？」曰：「修己以安百姓。修己以安百姓，尧舜其犹病诸！」

原壤夷俟。子曰：「幼而不孙弟，长而无述焉，老而不死，是为贼！」以杖叩其胫。

阙党童子将命。或问之曰：「益者与？」子曰：「吾见其居于位也，见其与先生并行也。非求益者也，欲速成者也。」

CHAP. XLIV. The Master said, 'When rulers love to observe the rules of propriety, the people respond readily to the calls on them for service.'

CHAP. XLV. Tsze-lu asked what constituted the superior man. The Master said, 'The cultivation of himself in reverential carefulness.' 'And is this all?' said Tsze-lu. 'He cultivates himself so as to give rest to others,' was the reply. 'And is this all?' again asked Tsze-lu. The Master said, 'He cultivates himself so as to give rest to all the people. He cultivates himself so as to give rest to all the people:— even Yao and Shun were still solicitous about this.'

CHAP. XLVI. Yuan Zang was squatting on his heels, and so waited the approach of the Master, who said to him, 'In youth not humble as befits a junior; in manhood, doing nothing worthy of being handed down; and living on to old age:— this is to be a pest.' With this he hit him on the shank with his staff.

CHAP. XLVI. 1. A youth of the village of Ch'ueh was employed by Confucius to carry the messages between him and his visitors. Some one asked about him, saying, 'I suppose he has made great progress.' 2. The Master said, 'I observe that he is fond of occupying the seat of a full-grown man; I observe that he walks shoulder to shoulder with his elders. He is not one who is seeking to make progress in learning. He wishes quickly to become a man.'

SEAL SCRIPT

衛靈公第十五

衛靈公問陳於孔子。孔子對曰:「俎豆之事,則嘗聞之矣;軍旅之事,未之學也。」明日遂行。

在陳絕糧,從者病,莫能興。子路慍見曰:「君子亦有窮乎?」子曰:「君子固窮,小人窮斯濫矣。」

子曰:「賜也,女以予為多學而識之者與?」對曰:「然,非與?」曰:「非也,予一以貫之。」

子曰:「由!知德者鮮矣。」

子曰:「無為而治者,其舜也與?夫何為哉,恭己正南面而已矣。」

卫灵公第十五

卫灵公问陈于孔子。孔子对曰:「俎豆之事,则尝闻之矣;军旅之事,未之学也。」明日遂行。

在陈绝粮,从者病,莫能兴。子路愠见曰:「君子亦有穷乎?」子曰:「君子固穷,小人穷斯滥矣。」

子曰:「赐也,女以予为多学而识之者与?」对曰:「然,非与?」曰:「非也,予一以贯之。」

子曰:「由!知德者鲜矣。」

子曰:「无为而治者,其舜也与?夫何为哉,恭己正南面而已矣。」

BOOK XV. WEI LING KUNG.

CHAP. I. 1. The Duke Ling of Wei asked Confucius about tactics. Confucius replied, 'I have heard all about sacrificial vessels, but I have not learned military matters.' On this, he took his departure the next day. 2. When he was in Chan, their provisions were exhausted, and his followers became so ill that they were unable to rise. 3. Tsze-lu, with evident dissatisfaction, said, 'Has the superior man likewise to endure in this way?' The Master said, 'The superior man may indeed have to endure want, but the mean man, when he is in want, gives way to unbridled license.'

CHAP. II. 1. The Master said, 'Ts'ze, you think, I suppose, that I am one who learns many things and keeps them in memory?' 2. Tsze-kung replied, 'Yes,—but perhaps it is not so?' 3. 'No,' was the answer; 'I seek a unity all-pervading.'

CHAP. III. The Master said, 'Yu, those who know virtue are few.'

CHAP. IV. The Master said, 'May not Shun be instanced as having governed efficiently without exertion? What did he do? He did nothing but gravely and reverently occupy his royal seat.'

SEAL SCRIPT

203

　　子張問行。子曰：「言忠信，行篤敬，雖蠻貊之邦行矣；言不忠信，行不篤敬，雖州里行乎哉？立，則見其參於前也；在輿，則見其倚於衡也。夫然後行。」子張書諸紳。

　　子曰：「直哉史魚！邦有道，如矢；邦無道，如矢。」君子哉蘧伯玉！邦有道，則仕；邦無道，則可卷而懷之。」

　　子曰：「可與言而不與之言，失人；不可與言而與之言，失言。知者不失人，亦不失言。」

　　子张问行。子曰：「言忠信，行笃敬，虽蛮貊之邦行矣；言不忠信，行不笃敬，虽州里行乎哉？立，则见其参于前也；在舆，则见其倚于衡也。夫然后行。」子张书诸绅。

　　子曰：「直哉史鱼！邦有道，如矢；邦无道，如矢。」君子哉蘧伯玉！邦有道，则仕；邦无道，则可卷而怀之。」

　　子曰：「可与言而不与之言，失人；不可与言而与之言，失言。知者不失人，亦不失言。」

CHAP. V. 1. Tsze-chang asked how a man should conduct himself, so as to be everywhere appreciated. 2. The Master said, 'Let his words be sincere and truthful, and his actions honourable and careful;— such conduct may be practised among the rude tribes of the South or the North. If his words be not sincere and truthful and his actions not honourable and careful, will he, with such conduct, be appreciated, even in his neighborhood? 3. 'When he is standing, let him see those two things, as it were, fronting him. When he is in a carriage, let him see them attached to the yoke. Then may he subsequently carry them into practice.' 4. Tsze-chang wrote these counsels on the end of his sash.

CHAP. VI. 1. The Master said, 'Truly straightforward was the historiographer Yu. When good government prevailed in his State, he was like an arrow. When bad government prevailed, he was like an arrow. 2. A superior man indeed is Chu Po-yu! When good government prevails in his state, he is to be found in office. When bad government prevails, he can roll his principles up, and keep them in his breast.'

CHAP. VII. The Master said, 'When a man may be spoken with, not to speak to him is to err in reference to the man. When a man may not be spoken with, to speak to him is to err in reference to our words. The wise err neither in regard to their man nor to their words.'

SEAL SCRIPT

子曰：「志士仁人，無求生以害仁，有殺身以成仁。」

子貢問為仁。子曰：「工欲善其事，必先利其器。居是邦也，事其大夫之賢者，友其士之仁者。」

顏淵問為邦。子曰：「行夏之時，乘殷之輅，服周之冕，樂則韶舞。放鄭聲，遠佞人。鄭聲淫，佞人殆。」

子曰：「人無遠慮，必有近憂。」

子曰：「已矣乎！吾未見好德如好色者也。」

子曰：「志士仁人，无求生以害仁，有杀身以成仁。」

子贡问为仁。子曰：「工欲善其事，必先利其器。居是邦也，事其大夫之贤者，友其士之仁者。」

颜渊问为邦。子曰：「行夏之时，乘殷之辂，服周之冕，乐则韶舞。放郑声，远佞人。郑声淫，佞人殆。」

子曰：「人无远虑，必有近忧。」

子曰：「已矣乎！吾未见好德如好色者也。」

CHAP. VIII. The Master said, 'The determined scholar and the man of virtue will not seek to live at the expense of injuring their virtue. They will even sacrifice their lives to preserve their virtue complete.'

CHAP. IX. Tsze-kung asked about the practice of virtue. The Master said, 'The mechanic, who wishes to do his work well, must first sharpen his tools. When you are living in any state, take service with the most worthy among its great officers, and make friends of the most virtuous among its scholars.'

CHAP. X. 1. Yen Yuan asked how the government of a country should be administered. 2. The Master said, 'Follow the seasons of Hsia. 3. 'Ride in the state carriage of Yin. 4. 'Wear the ceremonial cap of Chau. 5. 'Let the music be the Shao with its pantomimes. 6. Banish the songs of Chang, and keep far from specious talkers. The songs of Chang are licentious; specious talkers are dangerous.'

CHAP. XI. The Master said, 'If a man take no thought about what is distant, he will find sorrow near at hand.'

CHAP. XII. The Master said, 'It is all over! I have not seen one who loves virtue as he loves beauty.'

SEAL SCRIPT

207

子曰：「臧文仲其竊位者與？知柳下惠之賢，而不與立也。」

子曰：「躬自厚而薄責於人，則遠怨矣。」

子曰：「不曰『如之何如之何』者，吾末如之何也已矣。」

子曰：「群居終日，言不及義，好行小慧，難矣哉！」

子曰：「君子義以為質，禮以行之，孫以出之，信以成之。君子哉！」

子曰：「君子病無能焉，不病人之不己知也。」

子曰：「臧文仲其窃位者与？知柳下惠之贤，而不与立也。」

子曰：「躬自厚而薄责于人，则远怨矣。」

子曰：「不曰『如之何如之何』者，吾末如之何也已矣。」

子曰：「群居终日，言不及义，好行小慧，难矣哉！」

子曰：「君子义以为质，礼以行之，孙以出之，信以成之。君子哉！」

子曰：「君子病无能焉，不病人之不己知也。」

CHAP. XIII. The Master said, 'Was not Tsang Wan like one who had stolen his situation? He knew the virtue and the talents of Hui of Liu-hsia, and yet did not procure that he should stand with him in court.'

CHAP. XIV. The Master said, 'He who requires much from himself and little from others, will keep himself from being the object of resentment.'

CHAP. XV. The Master said, 'When a man is not in the habit of saying— "What shall I think of this? What shall I think of this?" I can indeed do nothing with him!'

CHAP. XVI. The Master said, 'When a number of people are together, for a whole day, without their conversation turning on righteousness, and when they are fond of carrying out the suggestions of a small shrewdness;— theirs is indeed a hard case.'

CHAP. XVII. The Master said, 'The superior man in everything considers righteousness to be essential. He performs it according to the rules of propriety. He brings it forth in humility. He completes it with sincerity. This is indeed a superior man.'

CHAP. XVIII. The Master said, 'The superior man is distressed by his want of ability. He is not distressed by men's not knowing him.'

SEAL SCRIPT

子曰：「君子疾沒世而名不稱焉。」

子曰：「君子求諸己，小人求諸人。」

子曰：「君子矜而不爭，群而不黨。」

子曰：「君子不以言舉人，不以人廢言。」

子貢問曰：「有一言而可以終身行之者乎？」子曰：「其恕乎！己所不欲，勿施於人。」

子曰：「吾之於人也，誰毀誰譽？如有所譽者，其有所試矣。斯民也，三代之所以直道而行也。」

子曰：「吾猶及史之闕文也，有馬者借人乘之。今亡矣夫！」

子曰：「君子疾没世而名不称焉。」

子曰：「君子求诸己，小人求诸人。」

子曰：「君子矜而不争，群而不党。」

子曰：「君子不以言举人，不以人废言。」

子贡问曰：「有一言而可以终身行之者乎？」子曰：「其恕乎！己所不欲，勿施于人。」

子曰：「吾之于人也，谁毁谁誉？如有所誉者，其有所试矣。斯民也，三代之所以直道而行也。」

子曰：「吾犹及史之阙文也，有马者借人乘之。今亡矣夫！」

CHAP. XIX. The Master said, 'The superior man dislikes the thought of his name not being mentioned after his death.'

CHAP. XX. The Master said, 'What the superior man seeks, is in himself. What the mean man seeks, is in others.'

CHAP. XXI. The Master said, 'The superior man is dignified, but does not wrangle. He is sociable, but not a partizan.'

CHAP. XXII. The Master said, 'The superior man does not promote a man simply on account of his words, nor does he put aside good words because of the man.'

CHAP. XXIII. Tsze-kung asked, saying, 'Is there one word which may serve as a rule of practice for all one's life?' The Master said, 'Is not RECIPROCITY such a word? What you do not want done to yourself, do not do to others.'

CHAP. XXIV. 1. The Master said, 'In my dealings with men, whose evil do I blame, whose goodness do I praise, beyond what is proper? If I do sometimes exceed in praise, there must be ground for it in my examination of the individual. 2. 'This people supplied the ground why the three dynasties pursued the path of straightforwardness.'

CHAP. XXV. The Master said, 'Even in my early days, a historiographer would leave a blank in his text, and he who had a horse would lend him to another to ride. Now, alas! there are no such things.'

SEAL SCRIPT

子曰：「巧言亂德，小不忍則亂大謀。」

子曰：「眾惡之，必察焉；眾好之，必察焉。」

子曰：「人能弘道，非道弘人。」

子曰：「過而不改，是謂過矣。」

子曰：「吾嘗終日不食，終夜不寢，以思，無益，不如學也。」

子曰：「君子謀道不謀食。耕也，餒在其中矣；學也，祿在其中矣。君子憂道不憂貧。」

子曰：「巧言乱德，小不忍则乱大谋。」

子曰：「众恶之，必察焉；众好之，必察焉。」

子曰：「人能弘道，非道弘人。」

子曰：「过而不改，是谓过矣。」

子曰：「吾尝终日不食，终夜不寝，以思，无益，不如学也。」

子曰：「君子谋道不谋食。耕也，馁在其中矣；学也，禄在其中矣。君子忧道不忧贫。」

CHAP. XXVI. The Master said, 'Specious words confound virtue. Want of forbearance in small matters confounds great plans.'

CHAP. XXVII. The Master said, 'When the multitude hate a man, it is necessary to examine into the case. When the multitude like a man, it is necessary to examine into the case.'

CHAP. XXVIII. The Master said, 'A man can enlarge the principles which he follows; those principles do not enlarge the man.'

CHAP. XXIX. The Master said, 'To have faults and not to reform them,— this, indeed, should be pronounced having faults.'

CHAP. XXX. The Master said, 'I have been the whole day without eating, and the whole night without sleeping:— occupied with thinking. It was of no use. The better plan is to learn.'

CHAP. XXXI. The Master said, 'The object of the superior man is truth. Food is not his object. There is plowing;— even in that there is sometimes want. So with learning;— emolument may be found in it. The superior man is anxious lest he should not get truth; he is not anxious lest poverty should come upon him.'

SEAL SCRIPT

子曰：「知及之，仁不能守之；雖得之，必失之。知及之，仁能守之。不莊以涖之，則民不敬。知及之，仁能守之，莊以涖之。動之不以禮，未善也。」

子曰：「君子不可小知，而可大受也；小人不可大受，而可小知也。」

子曰：「民之於仁也，甚於水火。水火，吾見蹈而死者矣，未見蹈仁而死者也。」

子曰：「當仁不讓於師。」

子曰：「君子貞而不諒。」

子曰：「事君，敬其事而後其食。」

子曰：「知及之，仁不能守之；虽得之，必失之。知及之，仁能守之。不庄以涖之，则民不敬。知及之，仁能守之，庄以涖之。动之不以礼，未善也。」

子曰：「君子不可小知，而可大受也；小人不可大受，而可小知也。」

子曰：「民之于仁也，甚于水火。水火，吾见蹈而死者矣，未见蹈仁而死者也。」

子曰：「当仁不让于师。」

子曰：「君子贞而不谅。」

子曰：「事君，敬其事而后其食。」

CHAP. XXXII. 1. The Master said, 'When a man's knowledge is sufficient to attain, and his virtue is not sufficient to enable him to hold, whatever he may have gained, he will lose again. 2. 'When his knowledge is sufficient to attain, and he has virtue enough to hold fast, if he cannot govern with dignity, the people will not respect him. 3. 'When his knowledge is sufficient to attain, and he has virtue enough to hold fast; when he governs also with dignity, yet if he try to move the people contrary to the rules of propriety:— full excellence is not reached.'

CHAP. XXXIII. The Master said, 'The superior man cannot be known in little matters; but he may be intrusted with great concerns. The small man may not be intrusted with great concerns, but he may be known in little matters.'

CHAP. XXXIV. The Master said, 'Virtue is more to man than either water or fire. I have seen men die from treading on water and fire, but I have never seen a man die from treading the course of virtue.'

CHAP. XXXV. The Master said, 'Let every man consider virtue as what devolves on himself. He may not yield the performance of it even to his teacher.'

CHAP. XXXVI. The Master said, 'The superior man is correctly firm, and not firm merely.'

CHAP. XXXVII. The Master said, 'A minister, in serving his prince, reverently discharges his duties, and makes his emolument a secondary consideration.'

SEAL SCRIPT

子曰：「有教無類。」

子曰：「道不同，不相為謀。」

子曰：「辭達而已矣。」

師冕見，及階，子曰：「階也。」及席，子曰：「席也。」皆坐，子告之曰：「某在斯，某在斯。」師冕出。子張問曰：「與師言之道與？」子曰：「然。固相師之道也。」

子曰：「有教无类。」

子曰：「道不同，不相为谋。」

子曰：「辞达而已矣。」

师冕见，及阶，子曰：「阶也。」及席，子曰：「席也。」皆坐，子告之曰：「某在斯，某在斯。」师冕出。子张问曰：「与师言之道与？」子曰：「然。固相师之道也。」

CHAP. XXXVIII. The Master said, 'In teaching there should be no distinction of classes.'

CHAP. XXXIX. The Master said, 'Those whose courses are different cannot lay plans for one another.'

CHAP. XL. The Master said, 'In language it is simply required that it convey the meaning.'

CHAP. XLI. 1. The Music-master, Mien, having called upon him, when they came to the steps, the Master said, 'Here are the steps.' When they came to the mat for the guest to sit upon, he said, 'Here is the mat.' When all were seated, the Master informed him, saying, 'So and so is here; so and so is here.' 2. The Music-master, Mien, having gone out, Tsze-chang asked, saying. 'Is it the rule to tell those things to the Music- master?' 3. The Master said, 'Yes. This is certainly the rule for those who lead the blind.'

SEAL SCRIPT

季氏第十六

　　季氏將伐顓臾。冉有、季路見於孔子曰：「季氏將有事於顓臾。」孔子曰：「求！無乃爾是過與？夫顓臾，昔者先王以為東蒙主，且在邦域之中矣，是社稷之臣也。何以伐為？」冉有曰：「夫子欲之，吾二臣者皆不欲也。」孔子曰：「求！周任有言曰：『陳力就列，不能者止。』危而不持，顛而不扶，則將焉用彼相矣？且爾言過矣。虎兕出於柙，龜玉毀於櫝中，是誰之過與？」冉有曰：「今夫顓臾，固而近於費。今不取，後世必為子孫憂。」孔子曰：「求！君子疾夫舍曰欲之，而必為之辭。丘也聞有國有家者，不患寡而患不均，不患貧而患不安。蓋均無貧，和無寡，安無傾。

季氏第十六

　　季氏将伐颛臾。冉有、季路见于孔子曰：「季氏将有事于颛臾。」孔子曰：「求！无乃尔是过与？夫颛臾，昔者先王以为东蒙主，且在邦域之中矣，是社稷之臣也。何以伐为？」冉有曰：「夫子欲之，吾二臣者皆不欲也。」孔子曰：「求！周任有言曰：『陈力就列，不能者止。』危而不持，颠而不扶，则将焉用彼相矣？且尔言过矣。虎兕出于柙，龟玉毁于椟中，是谁之过与？」冉有曰：「今夫颛臾，固而近于费。今不取，后世必为子孙忧。」孔子曰：「求！君子疾夫舍曰欲之，而必为之辞。丘也闻有国有家者，不患寡而患不均，不患贫而患不安。盖均无贫，和无寡，安无倾。

BOOK XVI. KE SHE.

CHAP. I. 1. The head of the Chi family was going to attack Chwan-yu. 2. Zan Yu and Chi-lu had an interview with Confucius, and said, 'Our chief, Chi, is going to commence operations against Chwan-yu.' 3. Confucius said, 'Ch'iu, is it not you who are in fault here? 4. 'Now, in regard to Chwan-yu, long ago, a former king appointed its ruler to preside over the sacrifices to the eastern Mang; moreover, it is in the midst of the territory of our State; and its ruler is a minister in direct connexion with the sovereign:— What has your chief to do with attacking it?' 5. Zan Yu said, 'Our master wishes the thing; neither of us two ministers wishes it.' 6. Confucius said, 'Ch'iu, there are the words of Chau Zan,— "When he can put forth his ability, he takes his place in the ranks of office; when he finds himself unable to do so, he retires from it. How can he be used as a guide to a blind man, who does not support him when tottering, nor raise him up when fallen?" 7. 'And further, you speak wrongly. When a tiger or rhinoceros escapes from his cage; when a tortoise or piece of jade is injured in its repository:— whose is the fault?' 8. Zan Yu said, 'But at present, Chwan-yu is strong and near to Pi; if our chief do not now take it, it will hereafter be a sorrow to his descendants.' 9. Confucius said. 'Ch'iu, the superior man hates that declining to say— "I want such and such a thing," and framing explanations for the conduct. 10. 'I have heard that rulers of States and chiefs of families are not troubled lest their people

SEAL SCRIPT

夫如是，故遠人不服，則修文德以來之。既來之，則安之。今由與求也，相夫子，遠人不服而不能來也；邦分崩離析而不能守也。而謀動干戈於邦內。吾恐季孫之憂，不在顓臾，而在蕭牆之內也。」

夫如是，故远人不服，则修文德以来之。既来之，则安之。今由与求也，相夫子，远人不服而不能来也；邦分崩离析而不能守也。而谋动干戈于邦内。吾恐季孙之忧，不在颛臾，而在萧墙之内也。」

should be few, but are troubled lest they should not keep their several places; that they are not troubled with fears of poverty, but are troubled with fears of a want of contented repose among the people in their several places. For when the people keep their several places, there will be no poverty; when harmony prevails, there will be no scarcity of people; and when there is such a contented repose, there will be no rebellious upsettings. 11. 'So it is.— Therefore, if remoter people are not submissive, all the influences of civil culture and virtue are to be cultivated to attract them to be so; and when they have been so attracted, they must be made contented and tranquil. 12. 'Now, here are you, Yu and Ch'iu, assisting your chief. Remoter people are not submissive, and, with your help, he cannot attract them to him. In his own territory there are divisions and downfalls, leavings and separations, and, with your help, he cannot preserve it. 13. 'And yet he is planning these hostile movements within the State.— I am afraid that the sorrow of the Chi-sun family will not be on account of Chwan-yu, but will be found within the screen of their own court.'

SEAL SCRIPT

　　孔子曰：「天下有道，則禮樂征伐自天子出；天下無道，則禮樂征伐自諸侯出。自諸侯出，蓋十世希不失矣；自大夫出，五世希不失矣；陪臣執國命，三世希不失矣。天下有道，則政不在大夫。天下有道，則庶人不議。」

　　孔子曰：「祿之去公室，五世矣；政逮於大夫，四世矣；故夫三桓之子孫，微矣。」

　　孔子曰：「天下有道，则礼乐征伐自天子出；天下无道，则礼乐征伐自诸侯出。自诸侯出，盖十世希不失矣；自大夫出，五世希不失矣；陪臣执国命，三世希不失矣。天下有道，则政不在大夫。天下有道，则庶人不议。」

　　孔子曰：「禄之去公室，五世矣；政逮于大夫，四世矣；故夫三桓之子孙，微矣。」

CHAP. II. 1. Confucius said, 'When good government prevails in the empire, ceremonies, music, and punitive military expeditions proceed from the son of Heaven. When bad government prevails in the empire, ceremonies, music, and punitive military expeditions proceed from the princes. When these things proceed from the princes, as a rule, the cases will be few in which they do not lose their power in ten generations. When they proceed from the Great officers of the princes, as a rule, the cases will be few in which they do not lose their power in five generations. When the subsidiary ministers of the great officers hold in their grasp the orders of the state, as a rule, the cases will be few in which they do not lose their power in three generations. 2. 'When right principles prevail in the kingdom, government will not be in the hands of the Great officers. 3. 'When right principles prevail in the kingdom, there will be no discussions among the common people.'

CHAP. III. Confucius said, 'The revenue of the state has left the ducal House now for five generations. The government has been in the hands of the Great officers for four generations. On this account, the descendants of the three Hwan are much reduced.'

SEAL SCRIPT

孔子曰:「益者三友，損者三友。友直，友諒，友多聞，益矣。友便辟，友善柔，友便佞，損矣。」

孔子曰:「益者三樂，損者三樂。樂節禮樂，樂道人之善，樂多賢友，益矣。樂驕樂，樂佚遊，樂宴樂，損矣。」

孔子曰:「侍於君子有三愆：言未及之而言謂之躁，言及之而不言謂之隱，未見顏色而言謂之瞽。」

孔子曰:「益者三友，损者三友。友直，友谅，友多闻，益矣。友便辟，友善柔，友便佞，损矣。」

孔子曰:「益者三乐，损者三乐。乐节礼乐，乐道人之善，乐多贤友，益矣。乐骄乐，乐佚游，乐宴乐，损矣。」

孔子曰:「侍于君子有三愆：言未及之而言谓之躁，言及之而不言谓之隐，未见颜色而言谓之瞽。」

CHAP. IV. Confucius said, 'There are three friendships which are advantageous, and three which are injurious. Friendship with the upright; friendship with the sincere; and friendship with the man of much observation:— these are advantageous. Friendship with the man of specious airs; friendship with the insinuatingly soft; and friendship with the glib-tongued:— these are injurious.'

CHAP. V. Confucius said, 'There are three things men find enjoyment in which are advantageous, and three things they find enjoyment in which are injurious. To find enjoyment in the discriminating study of ceremonies and music; to find enjoyment in speaking of the goodness of others; to find enjoyment in having many worthy friends:— these are advantageous. To find enjoyment in extravagant pleasures; to find enjoyment in idleness and sauntering; to find enjoyment in the pleasures of feasting:— these are injurious.'

CHAP. VI. Confucius said, 'There are three errors to which they who stand in the presence of a man of virtue and station are liable. They may speak when it does not come to them to speak;— this is called rashness. They may not speak when it comes to them to speak;— this is called concealment. They may speak without looking at the countenance of their superior;— this is called blindness.'

SEAL SCRIPT

　　孔子曰：「君子有三戒：少之時，血氣未定，戒之在色；及其壯也，血氣方剛，戒之在鬪；及其老也，血氣既衰，戒之在得。」

　　孔子曰：「君子有三畏：畏天命，畏大人，畏聖人之言。小人不知天命而不畏也，狎大人，侮聖人之言。」

　　孔子曰：「生而知之者，上也；學而知之者，次也；困而學之，又其次也；困而不學，民斯為下矣。」

　　孔子曰：「君子有三戒：少之时，血气未定，戒之在色；及其壮也，血气方刚，戒之在鬪；及其老也，血气既衰，戒之在得。」

　　孔子曰：「君子有三畏：畏天命，畏大人，畏圣人之言。小人不知天命而不畏也，狎大人，侮圣人之言。」

　　孔子曰：「生而知之者，上也；学而知之者，次也；困而学之，又其次也；困而不学，民斯为下矣。」

CHAP. VII. Confucius said, 'There are three things which the superior man guards against. In youth, when the physical powers are not yet settled, he guards against lust. When he is strong and the physical powers are full of vigor, he guards against quarrelsomeness. When he is old, and the animal powers are decayed, he guards against covetousness.'

CHAP. VIII. 1. Confucius said, 'There are three things of which the superior man stands in awe. He stands in awe of the ordinances of Heaven. He stands in awe of great men. He stands in awe of the words of sages. 2. 'The mean man does not know the ordinances of Heaven, and consequently does not stand in awe of them. He is disrespectful to great men. He makes sport of the words of sages.'

CHAP. IX. Confucius said, 'Those who are born with the possession of knowledge are the highest class of men. Those who learn, and so, readily, get possession of knowledge, are the next. Those who are dull and stupid, and yet compass the learning, are another class next to these. As to those who are dull and stupid and yet do not learn;— they are the lowest of the people.'

SEAL SCRIPT

孔子曰：「君子有九思：視思明，聽思聰，色思溫，貌思恭，言思忠，事思敬，疑思問，忿思難，見得思義。」

孔子曰：「見善如不及，見不善如探湯。吾見其人矣，吾聞其語矣。隱居以求其志，行義以達其道。吾聞其語矣，未見其人也。」

孔子曰：「君子有九思：视思明，听思聪，色思温，貌思恭，言思忠，事思敬，疑思问，忿思难，见得思义。」

孔子曰：「见善如不及，见不善如探汤。吾见其人矣，吾闻其语矣。隐居以求其志，行义以达其道。吾闻其语矣，未见其人也。」

CHAP. X. Confucius said, 'The superior man has nine things which are subjects with him of thoughtful consideration. In regard to the use of his eyes, he is anxious to see clearly. In regard to the use of his ears, he is anxious to hear distinctly. In regard to his countenance, he is anxious that it should be benign. In regard to his demeanor, he is anxious that it should be respectful. In regard to his speech, he is anxious that it should be sincere. In regard to his doing of business, he is anxious that it should be reverently careful. In regard to what he doubts about, he is anxious to question others. When he is angry, he thinks of the difficulties (his anger may involve him in). When he sees gain to be got, he thinks of righteousness.'

CHAP. XI. 1. Confucius said, 'Contemplating good, and pursuing it, as if they could not reach it; contemplating evil, and shrinking from it, as they would from thrusting the hand into boiling water:— I have seen such men, as I have heard such words. 2. 'Living in retirement to study their aims, and practising righteousness to carry out their principles:— I have heard these words, but I have not seen such men.'

SEAL SCRIPT

齊景公有馬千駟，死之日，民無德而稱焉。伯夷叔齊餓于首陽之下，民到于今稱之。其斯之謂與？

陳亢問於伯魚曰：「子亦有異聞乎？」對曰：「未也。嘗獨立，鯉趨而過庭。曰：『學詩乎？』對曰：『未也。』『不學詩，無以言。』鯉退而學詩。他日又獨立，鯉趨而過庭。曰：『學禮乎？』對曰：『未也。』『不學禮，無以立。』鯉退而學禮。聞斯二者。」陳亢退而喜曰：「問一得三，聞詩，聞禮，又聞君子之遠其子也。」

齐景公有马千驷，死之日，民无德而称焉。伯夷叔齐饿于首阳之下，民到于今称之。其斯之谓与？

陈亢问于伯鱼曰：「子亦有异闻乎？」对曰：「未也。尝独立，鲤趋而过庭。曰：『学诗乎？』对曰：『未也。』『不学诗，无以言。』鲤退而学诗。他日又独立，鲤趋而过庭。曰：『学礼乎？』对曰：『未也。』『不学礼，无以立。』鲤退而学礼。闻斯二者。」陈亢退而喜曰：「问一得三，闻诗，闻礼，又闻君子之远其子也。」

CHAP. XII. 1. The duke Ching of Ch'i had a thousand teams, each of four horses, but on the day of his death, the people did not praise him for a single virtue. Po-i and Shu-ch'i died of hunger at the foot of the Shau-yang mountain, and the people, down to the present time, praise them. 2. 'Is not that saying illustrated by this?'

CHAP. XIII. 1. Ch'an K'ang asked Po-yu, saying, 'Have you heard any lessons from your father different from what we have all heard?' 2. Po-yu replied, 'No. He was standing alone once, when I passed below the hall with hasty steps, and said to me, "Have you learned the Odes?" On my replying "Not yet," he added, "If you do not learn the Odes, you will not be fit to converse with." I retired and studied the Odes. 3. 'Another day, he was in the same way standing alone, when I passed by below the hall with hasty steps, and said to me, 'Have you learned the rules of Propriety?' On my replying 'Not yet,' he added, 'If you do not learn the rules of Propriety, your character cannot be established.' I then retired, and learned the rules of Propriety. 4. 'I have heard only these two things from him.' 5. Ch'ang K'ang retired, and, quite delighted, said, 'I asked one thing, and I have got three things. I have heard about the Odes. I have heard about the rules of Propriety. I have also heard that the superior man maintains a distant reserve towards his son.'

SEAL SCRIPT

　　邦君之妻，君稱之曰夫人，夫人自稱曰小童；邦人稱之曰君夫人，稱諸異邦曰寡小君；異邦人稱之亦曰君夫人。

　　邦君之妻，君称之曰夫人，夫人自称曰小童；邦人称之曰君夫人，称诸异邦曰寡小君；异邦人称之亦曰君夫人。

CHAP. XIV. The wife of the prince of a state is called by him FU ZAN. She calls herself HSIAO T'UNG. The people of the State call her CHUN FU ZAN, and, to the people of other States, they call her K'WA HSIAO CHUN. The people of other states also call her CHUN FU ZAN.

SEAL SCRIPT

陽貨第十七

　　陽貨欲見孔子，孔子不見，歸孔子豚。孔子時其亡也，而往拜之，遇諸塗。謂孔子曰：「來！予與爾言。」曰：「懷其寶而迷其邦，可謂仁乎？」曰：「不可。」「好從事而亟失時，可謂知乎？」曰：「不可。」「日月逝矣，歲不我與。」孔子曰：「諾。吾將仕矣。」

　　子曰：「性相近也，習相遠也。」

　　子曰：「唯上知與下愚不移。」

阳货第十七

　　阳货欲见孔子，孔子不见，归孔子豚。孔子时其亡也，而往拜之，遇诸涂。谓孔子曰：「来！予与尔言。」曰：「怀其宝而迷其邦，可谓仁乎？」曰：「不可。」「好从事而亟失时，可谓知乎？」曰：「不可。」「日月逝矣，岁不我与。」孔子曰：「诺。吾将仕矣。」

　　子曰：「性相近也，习相远也。」

　　子曰：「唯上知与下愚不移。」

BOOK XVII. YANG HO.

CHAP. I. 1. Yang Ho wished to see Confucius, but Confucius would not go to see him. On this, he sent a present of a pig to Confucius, who, having chosen a time when Ho was not at home, went to pay his respects for the gift. He met him, however, on the way. 2. Ho said to Confucius, 'Come, let me speak with you.' He then asked, 'Can he be called benevolent who keeps his jewel in his bosom, and leaves his country to confusion?' Confucius replied, 'No.' 'Can he be called wise, who is anxious to be engaged in public employment, and yet is constantly losing the opportunity of being so?' Confucius again said, 'No.' 'The days and months are passing away; the years do not wait for us.' Confucius said, 'Right; I will go into office.'

CHAP. II. The Master said, 'By nature, men are nearly alike; by practice, they get to be wide apart.'

CHAP. III. The Master said, 'There are only the wise of the highest class, and the stupid of the lowest class, who cannot be changed.'

SEAL SCRIPT

235

子之武城，聞弦歌之聲。夫子莞爾而笑，曰：「割雞焉用牛刀？」子游對曰：「昔者偃也聞諸夫子曰：『君子學道則愛人，小人學道則易使也。』」子曰：「二三子！偃之言是也。前言戲之耳。」

公山弗擾以費畔，召，子欲往。子路不說，曰：「末之也已，何必公山氏之之也。」子曰：「夫召我者而豈徒哉？如有用我者，吾其為東周乎？」

子張問仁於孔子。孔子曰：「能行五者於天下，為仁矣。」請問之。曰：「恭、寬、信、敏、惠。恭則不侮，寬則得眾，信則人任焉，敏則有功，惠則足以使人。」

子之武城，闻弦歌之声。夫子莞尔而笑，曰：「割鸡焉用牛刀？」子游对曰：「昔者偃也闻诸夫子曰：『君子学道则爱人，小人学道则易使也。』」子曰：「二三子！偃之言是也。前言戏之耳。」

公山弗扰以费畔，召，子欲往。子路不说，曰：「末之也已，何必公山氏之之也。」子曰：「夫召我者而岂徒哉？如有用我者，吾其为东周乎？」

子张问仁于孔子。孔子曰：「能行五者于天下，为仁矣。」请问之。曰：「恭、宽、信、敏、惠。恭则不侮，宽则得众，信则人任焉，敏则有功，惠则足以使人。」

CHAP. IV. 1. The Master, having come to Wu-ch'ang, heard there the sound of stringed instruments and singing. 2. Well pleased and smiling, he said, 'Why use an ox knife to kill a fowl?' 3. Tsze-yu replied, 'Formerly, Master, I heard you say,— "When the man of high station is well instructed, he loves men; when the man of low station is well instructed, he is easily ruled."' 4. The Master said, 'My disciples, Yen's words are right. What I said was only in sport.'

CHAP. V. Kung-shan Fu-zao, when he was holding Pi, and in an attitude of rebellion, invited the Master to visit him, who was rather inclined to go. 2. Tsze-lu was displeased, and said, 'Indeed, you cannot go! Why must you think of going to see Kung-shan?' 3. The Master said, 'Can it be without some reason that he has invited ME? If any one employ me, may I not make an eastern Chau?'

CHAP. VI. Tsze-chang asked Confucius about perfect virtue. Confucius said, 'To be able to practise five things everywhere under heaven constitutes perfect virtue.' He begged to ask what they were, and was told, 'Gravity, generosity of soul, sincerity, earnestness, and kindness. If you are grave, you will not be treated with disrespect. If you are generous, you will win all. If you are sincere, people will repose trust in you. If you are earnest, you will accomplish much. If you are kind, this will enable you to employ the services of others.

SEAL SCRIPT

　　佛肸召，子欲往。子路曰：「昔者由也聞諸夫子曰：『親於其身為不善者，君子不入也。』佛肸以中牟畔，子之往也，如之何！」子曰：「然。有是言也。不曰堅乎，磨而不磷；不曰白乎，涅而不緇。吾豈匏瓜也哉？焉能繫而不食？」

　　子曰：「由也，女聞六言六蔽矣乎？」對曰：「未也。」「居！吾語女。好仁不好學，其蔽也愚；好知不好學，其蔽也蕩；好信不好學，其蔽也賊；好直不好學，其蔽也絞；好勇不好學，其蔽也亂；好剛不好學，其蔽也狂。」

　　佛肸召，子欲往。子路曰：「昔者由也闻诸夫子曰：『亲于其身为不善者，君子不入也。』佛肸以中牟畔，子之往也，如之何！」子曰：「然。有是言也。不曰坚乎，磨而不磷；不曰白乎，涅而不缁。吾岂匏瓜也哉？焉能系而不食？」

　　子曰：「由也，女闻六言六蔽矣乎？」对曰：「未也。」「居！吾语女。好仁不好学，其蔽也愚；好知不好学，其蔽也荡；好信不好学，其蔽也贼；好直不好学，其蔽也绞；好勇不好学，其蔽也乱；好刚不好学，其蔽也狂。」

CHAP. VII. 1. Pi Hsi inviting him to visit him, the Master was inclined to go. 2. Tsze-lu said, 'Master, formerly I have heard you say, "When a man in his own person is guilty of doing evil, a superior man will not associate with him." Pi Hsi is in rebellion, holding possession of Chung-mau; if you go to him, what shall be said?' 3. The Master said, 'Yes, I did use these words. But is it not said, that, if a thing be really hard, it may be ground without being made thin? Is it not said, that, if a thing be really white, it may be steeped in a dark fluid without being made black? 4. 'Am I a bitter gourd! How can I be hung up out of the way of being eaten?'

CHAP. VIII. 1. The Master said, 'Yu, have you heard the six words to which are attached six becloudings?' Yu replied, 'I have not.' 2. 'Sit down, and I will tell them to you. 3. 'There is the love of being benevolent without the love of learning;— the beclouding here leads to a foolish simplicity. There is the love of knowing without the love of learning;— the beclouding here leads to dissipation of mind. There is the love of being sincere without the love of learning;— the beclouding here leads to an injurious disregard of consequences. There is the love of straightforwardness without the love of learning;— the beclouding here leads to rudeness. There is the love of boldness without the love of learning;— the beclouding here leads to insubordination. There is the love of firmness without the love of learning;— the beclouding here leads to extravagant conduct.'

SEAL SCRIPT

　　子曰：「小子！何莫學夫詩？詩，可以興，可以觀，可以群，可以怨。邇之事父，遠之事君。多識於鳥獸草木之名。」

　　子謂伯魚曰：「女為《周南》、《召南》矣乎？人而不為《周南》、《召南》，其猶正牆面而立也與？」

　　子曰：「禮云禮云，玉帛云乎哉？樂云樂云，鐘鼓云乎哉？」

　　子曰：「小子！何莫学夫诗？诗，可以兴，可以观，可以群，可以怨。迩之事父，远之事君。多识于鸟兽草木之名。」

　　子谓伯鱼曰：「女为《周南》、《召南》矣乎？人而不为《周南》、《召南》，其犹正墙面而立也与？」

　　子曰：「礼云礼云，玉帛云乎哉？乐云乐云，钟鼓云乎哉？」

CHAP. IX. 1. The Master said, 'My children, why do you not study the Book of Poetry? 2. 'The Odes serve to stimulate the mind. 3. 'They may be used for purposes of self-contemplation. 4. 'They teach the art of sociability. 5. 'They show how to regulate feelings of resentment. 6. 'From them you learn the more immediate duty of serving one's father, and the remoter one of serving one's prince. 7. 'From them we become largely acquainted with the names of birds, beasts, and plants.'

CHAP. X. The Master said to Po-yu, 'Do you give yourself to the Chau-nan and the Shao-nan. The man who has not studied the Chau-nan and the Shao-nan, is like one who stands with his face right against a wall. Is he not so?'

CHAP. XI. The Master said, '"It is according to the rules of propriety," they say.— "It is according to the rules of propriety," they say. Are gems and silk all that is meant by propriety? "It is music," they say.— "It is music," they say. Are bells and drums all that is meant by music?'

SEAL SCRIPT

子曰：「色厲而內荏，譬諸小人，其猶穿窬之盜也與？」

子曰：「鄉原，德之賊也。」

子曰：「道聽而塗說，德之棄也。」

子曰：「鄙夫！可與事君也與哉？其未得之也，患得之；既得之，患失之。苟患失之，無所不至矣。」

子曰：「古者民有三疾，今也或是之亡也。古之狂也肆，今之狂也蕩；古之矜也廉，今之矜也忿戾；古之愚也直，今之愚也詐而已矣。」

子曰：「色厉而内荏，譬诸小人，其犹穿窬之盗也与？」

子曰：「乡原，德之贼也。」

子曰：「道听而涂说，德之弃也。」

子曰：「鄙夫！可与事君也与哉？其未得之也，患得之；既得之，患失之。苟患失之，无所不至矣。」

子曰：「古者民有三疾，今也或是之亡也。古之狂也肆，今之狂也荡；古之矜也廉，今之矜也忿戾；古之愚也直，今之愚也诈而已矣。」

CHAP. XII. The Master said, 'He who puts on an appearance of stern firmness, while inwardly he is weak, is like one of the small, mean people;— yea, is he not like the thief who breaks through, or climbs over, a wall?'

CHAP. XIII. The Master said, 'Your good, careful people of the villages are the thieves of virtue.'

CHAP. XIV. The Master said, 'To tell, as we go along, what we have heard on the way, is to cast away our virtue.'

CHAP. XV. 1. The Master said, 'There are those mean creatures! How impossible it is along with them to serve one's prince! 2. 'While they have not got their aims, their anxiety is how to get them. When they have got them, their anxiety is lest they should lose them. 3. 'When they are anxious lest such things should be lost, there is nothing to which they will not proceed.'

CHAP. XVI. 1. The Master said, 'Anciently, men had three failings, which now perhaps are not to be found. 2. 'The high-mindedness of antiquity showed itself in a disregard of small things; the high-mindedness of the present day shows itself in wild license. The stern dignity of antiquity showed itself in grave reserve; the stern dignity of the present day shows itself in quarrelsome perverseness. The stupidity of antiquity showed itself in straightforwardness; the stupidity of the present day shows itself in sheer deceit.'

SEAL SCRIPT

243

　　子曰：「巧言令色，鮮矣仁。」

　　子曰：「惡紫之奪朱也，惡鄭聲之亂雅樂也，惡利口之覆邦家者。」

　　子曰：「予欲無言。」子貢曰：「子如不言，則小子何述焉？」子曰：「天何言哉？四時行焉，百物生焉，天何言哉？」

　　孺悲欲見孔子，孔子辭以疾。將命者出戶，取瑟而歌。使之聞之。

　　子曰：「巧言令色，鲜矣仁。」

　　子曰：「恶紫之夺朱也，恶郑声之乱雅乐也，恶利口之覆邦家者。」

　　子曰：「予欲无言。」子贡曰：「子如不言，则小子何述焉？」子曰：「天何言哉？四时行焉，百物生焉，天何言哉？」

　　孺悲欲见孔子，孔子辞以疾。将命者出户，取瑟而歌。使之闻之。

CHAP. XVII. The Master said, 'Fine words and an insinuating appearance are seldom associated with virtue.'

CHAP. XVIII. The Master said, 'I hate the manner in which purple takes away the luster of vermilion. I hate the way in which the songs of Chang confound the music of the Ya. I hate those who with their sharp mouths overthrow kingdoms and families.'

CHAP. XIX. 1. The Master said, 'I would prefer not speaking.' 2. Tsze-kung said, 'If you, Master, do not speak, what shall we, your disciples, have to record?' 3. The Master said, 'Does Heaven speak? The four seasons pursue their courses, and all things are continually being produced, but does Heaven say anything?'

CHAP. XX. Zu Pei wished to see Confucius, but Confucius declined, on the ground of being sick, to see him. When the bearer of this message went out at the door, (the Master) took his lute and sang to it, in order that Pei might hear him.

SEAL SCRIPT

宰我問：「三年之喪，期已久矣。君子三年不為禮，禮必壞；三年不為樂，樂必崩。舊穀既沒，新穀既升，鑽燧改火，期可已矣。」子曰：「食夫稻，衣夫錦，於女安乎？」曰：「安。」「女安則為之！夫君子之居喪，食旨不甘，聞樂不樂，居處不安，故不為也。今女安，則為之！」宰我出。子曰：「予之不仁也！子生三年，然後免於父母之懷。夫三年之喪，天下之通喪也。予也，有三年之愛於其父母乎？」

宰我问：「三年之丧，期已久矣。君子三年不为礼，礼必坏；三年不为乐，乐必崩。旧谷既没，新谷既升，钻燧改火，期可已矣。」子曰：「食夫稻，衣夫锦，于女安乎？」曰：「安。」「女安则为之！夫君子之居丧，食旨不甘，闻乐不乐，居处不安，故不为也。今女安，则为之！」宰我出。子曰：「予之不仁也！子生三年，然后免于父母之怀。夫三年之丧，天下之通丧也。予也，有三年之爱于其父母乎？」

CHAP. XXI. 1. Tsai Wo asked about the three years' mourning for parents, saying that one year was long enough. 2. 'If the superior man,' said he, 'abstains for three years from the observances of propriety, those observances will be quite lost. If for three years he abstains from music, music will be ruined. 3. 'Within a year the old grain is exhausted, and the new grain has sprung up, and, in procuring fire by friction, we go through all the changes of wood for that purpose. After a complete year, the mourning may stop.' 4. The Master said, 'If you were, after a year, to eat good rice, and wear embroidered clothes, would you feel at ease?' 'I should,' replied Wo. 5. The Master said, 'If you can feel at ease, do it. But a superior man, during the whole period of mourning, does not enjoy pleasant food which he may eat, nor derive pleasure from music which he may hear. He also does not feel at ease, if he is comfortably lodged. Therefore he does not do what you propose. But now you feel at ease and may do it.' 6. Tsai Wo then went out, and the Master said, 'This shows Yu's want of virtue. It is not till a child is three years old that it is allowed to leave the arms of its parents. And the three years' mourning is universally observed throughout the empire. Did Yu enjoy the three years' love of his parents?'

SEAL SCRIPT

子曰：「飽食終日，無所用心，難矣哉！不有博弈者乎，為之猶賢乎已。」

子路曰：「君子尚勇乎？」子曰：「君子義以為上。君子有勇而無義為亂，小人有勇而無義為盜。」

子貢曰：「君子亦有惡乎？」子曰：「有惡：惡稱人之惡者，惡居下流而訕上者，惡勇而無禮者，惡果敢而窒者。」曰：「賜也亦有惡乎？」「惡徼以為知者，惡不孫以為勇者，惡訐以為直者。」

子曰：「饱食终日，无所用心，难矣哉！不有博弈者乎，为之犹贤乎已。」

子路曰：「君子尚勇乎？」子曰：「君子义以为上。君子有勇而无义为乱，小人有勇而无义为盗。」

子贡曰：「君子亦有恶乎？」子曰：「有恶：恶称人之恶者，恶居下流而讪上者，恶勇而无礼者，恶果敢而窒者。」曰：「赐也亦有恶乎？」「恶徼以为知者，恶不孙以为勇者，恶讦以为直者。」

CHAP. XXII. The Master said, 'Hard is it to deal with him, who will stuff himself with food the whole day, without applying his mind to anything good! Are there not gamesters and chess players? To be one of these would still be better than doing nothing at all.'

CHAP. XXIII. Tsze-lu said, 'Does the superior man esteem valour?' The Master said, 'The superior man holds righteousness to be of highest importance. A man in a superior situation, having valour without righteousness, will be guilty of insubordination; one of the lower people having valour without righteousness, will commit robbery.'

CHAP. XXIV. 1. Tsze-kung said, 'Has the superior man his hatreds also?' The Master said, 'He has his hatreds. He hates those who proclaim the evil of others. He hates the man who, being in a low station, slanders his superiors. He hates those who have valour merely, and are unobservant of propriety. He hates those who are forward and determined, and, at the same time, of contracted understanding.' 2. The Master then inquired, 'Ts'ze, have you also your hatreds?' Tsze-kung replied, 'I hate those who pry out matters, and ascribe the knowledge to their wisdom. I hate those who are only not modest, and think that they are valourous. I hate those who make known secrets, and think that they are straightforward.'

SEAL SCRIPT

子曰：「唯女子與小人為難養也，近之則不孫，遠之則怨。」
子曰：「年四十而見惡焉，其終也已。」

子曰：「唯女子与小人为难养也，近之则不孙，远之则怨。」
子曰：「年四十而见恶焉，其终也已。」

CHAP. XXV. The Master said, 'Of all people, girls and servants are the most difficult to behave to. If you are familiar with them, they lose their humility. If you maintain a reserve towards them, they are discontented.'

CHAP. XXVI. The Master said, 'When a man at forty is the object of dislike, he will always continue what he is.'

SEAL SCRIPT

微子第十八

微子去之，箕子為之奴，比干諫而死。孔子曰：「殷有三仁焉。」

柳下惠為士師，三黜。人曰：「子未可以去乎？」曰：「直道而事人，焉往而不三黜？枉道而事人，何必去父母之邦。」

齊景公待孔子，曰：「若季氏則吾不能，以季、孟之閒待之。」曰：「吾老矣，不能用也。」孔子行。

齊人歸女樂，季桓子受之。三日不朝，孔子行。

SIMPLIFIED CHINESE

微子第十八

微子去之，箕子为之奴，比干谏而死。孔子曰：「殷有三仁焉。」

柳下惠为士师，三黜。人曰：「子未可以去乎？」曰：「直道而事人，焉往而不三黜？枉道而事人，何必去父母之邦。」

齐景公待孔子，曰：「若季氏则吾不能，以季、孟之闲待之。」曰：「吾老矣，不能用也。」孔子行。

齐人归女乐，季桓子受之。三日不朝，孔子行。

BOOK XVIII. WEI TSZE.

CHAP. I. 1. The Viscount of Wei withdrew from the court. The Viscount of Chi became a slave to Chau. Pi-kan remonstrated with him and died. 2. Confucius said, 'The Yin dynasty possessed these three men of virtue.'

CHAP. II. Hui of Liu-hsia being chief criminal judge, was thrice dismissed from his office. Some one said to him, 'Is it not yet time for you, sir, to leave this?' He replied, 'Serving men in an upright way, where shall I go to, and not experience such a thrice- repeated dismissal? If I choose to serve men in a crooked way, what necessity is there for me to leave the country of my parents?'

CHAP. III. The duke Ching of Ch'i, with reference to the manner in which he should treat Confucius, said, 'I cannot treat him as I would the chief of the Chi family. I will treat him in a manner between that accorded to the chief of the Chi, and that given to the chief of the Mang family.' He also said, 'I am old; I cannot use his doctrines.' Confucius took his departure.

CHAP. IV. The people of Ch'i sent to Lu a present of female musicians, which Chi Hwan received, and for three days no court was held. Confucius took his departure.

SEAL SCRIPT

　　楚狂接輿歌而過孔子曰：「鳳兮！鳳兮！何德之衰？往者不可諫，來者猶可追。已而，已而！今之從政者殆而！」孔子下，欲與之言。趨而辟之，不得與之言。

　　楚狂接輿歌而过孔子曰：「凤兮！凤兮！何德之衰？往者不可谏，来者犹可追。已而，已而！今之从政者殆而！」孔子下，欲与之言。趋而辟之，不得与之言。

CHAP. V. 1. The madman of Ch'u, Chieh-yu, passed by Confucius, singing and saying, 'O FANG! O FANG! How is your virtue degenerated! As to the past, reproof is useless; but the future may still be provided against. Give up your vain pursuit. Give up your vain pursuit. Peril awaits those who now engage in affairs of government.' 2. Confucius alighted and wished to converse with him, but Chieh-yu hastened away, so that he could not talk with him.

SEAL SCRIPT

　　長沮、桀溺耦而耕，孔子過之，使子路問津焉。長沮曰:「夫執輿者為誰?」子路曰:「為孔丘。」曰:「是魯孔丘與?」曰:「是也。」曰:「是知津矣。」問於桀溺，桀溺曰:「子為誰?」曰:「為仲由。」曰:「是魯孔丘之徒與?」對曰:「然。」曰:「滔滔者天下皆是也，而誰以易之?且而與其從辟人之士也，豈若從辟世之士哉?」耰而不輟。子路行以告。夫子憮然曰:「鳥獸不可與同群，吾非斯人之徒與而誰與?天下有道，丘不與易也。」

　　长沮、桀溺耦而耕，孔子过之，使子路问津焉。长沮曰:「夫执舆者为谁?」子路曰:「为孔丘。」曰:「是鲁孔丘与?」曰:「是也。」曰:「是知津矣。」问于桀溺，桀溺曰:「子为谁?」曰:「为仲由。」曰:「是鲁孔丘之徒与?」对曰:「然。」曰:「滔滔者天下皆是也，而谁以易之?且而与其从辟人之士也，岂若从辟世之士哉?」耰而不辍。子路行以告。夫子怃然曰:「鸟兽不可与同群，吾非斯人之徒与而谁与?天下有道，丘不与易也。」

CHAP. VI. 1. Ch'ang-tsu and Chieh-ni were at work in the field together, when Confucius passed by them, and sent Tsze-lu to inquire for the ford. 2. Ch'ang-tsu said, 'Who is he that holds the reins in the carriage there?' Tsze-lu told him, 'It is K'ung Ch'iu.' 'Is it not K'ung Ch'iu of Lu?' asked he. 'Yes,' was the reply, to which the other rejoined, 'He knows the ford.' 3. Tsze-lu then inquired of Chieh-ni, who said to him, 'Who are you, sir?' He answered, 'I am Chung Yu.' 'Are you not the disciple of K'ung Ch'iu of Lu?' asked the other. 'I am,' replied he, and then Chieh-ni said to him, 'Disorder, like a swelling flood, spreads over the whole empire, and who is he that will change its state for you? Than follow one who merely withdraws from this one and that one, had you not better follow those who have withdrawn from the world altogether?' With this he fell to covering up the seed, and proceeded with his work, without stopping. 4. Tsze-lu went and reported their remarks, when the Master observed with a sigh, 'It is impossible to associate with birds and beasts, as if they were the same with us. If I associate not with these people,— with mankind,— with whom shall I associate? If right principles prevailed through the empire, there would be no use for me to change its state.'

SEAL SCRIPT

　　子路從而後，遇丈人，以杖荷蓧。子路問曰：「子見夫子乎？」丈人曰：「四體不勤，五穀不分。孰為夫子？」植其杖而芸。子路拱而立。止子路宿，殺雞為黍而食之，見其二子焉。明日，子路行以告。子曰：「隱者也。」使子路反見之。至則行矣。子路曰：「不仕無義。長幼之節，不可廢也；君臣之義，如之何其廢之？欲潔其身，而亂大倫。君子之仕也，行其義也。道之不行，已知之矣。」

　　子路从而后，遇丈人，以杖荷蓧。子路问曰：「子见夫子乎？」丈人曰：「四体不勤，五谷不分。孰为夫子？」植其杖而芸。子路拱而立。止子路宿，杀鸡为黍而食之，见其二子焉。明日，子路行以告。子曰：「隐者也。」使子路反见之。至则行矣。子路曰：「不仕无义。长幼之节，不可废也；君臣之义，如之何其废之？欲洁其身，而乱大伦。君子之仕也，行其义也。道之不行，已知之矣。」

CHAP. VII. 1. Tsze-lu, following the Master, happened to fall behind, when he met an old man, carrying across his shoulder on a staff a basket for weeds. Tsze-lu said to him, 'Have you seen my master, sir!' The old man replied, 'Your four limbs are unaccustomed to toil; you cannot distinguish the five kinds of grain:— who is your master?' With this, he planted his staff in the ground, and proceeded to weed. 2. Tsze-lu joined his hands across his breast, and stood before him. 3. The old man kept Tsze-lu to pass the night in his house, killed a fowl, prepared millet, and feasted him. He also introduced to him his two sons. 4. Next day, Tsze-lu went on his way, and reported his adventure. The Master said, 'He is a recluse,' and sent Tsze-lu back to see him again, but when he got to the place, the old man was gone. 5. Tsze-lu then said to the family, 'Not to take office is not righteous. If the relations between old and young may not be neglected, how is it that he sets aside the duties that should be observed between sovereign and minister? Wishing to maintain his personal purity, he allows that great relation to come to confusion. A superior man takes office, and performs the righteous duties belonging to it. As to the failure of right principles to make progress, he is aware of that.'

SEAL SCRIPT

逸民:伯夷、叔齊、虞仲、夷逸、朱張、柳下惠、少連。子曰:「不降其志,不辱其身,伯夷、叔齊與!」謂:「柳下惠、少連,降志辱身矣。言中倫,行中慮,其斯而已矣。」謂:「虞仲、夷逸,隱居放言。身中清,廢中權。」「我則異於是,無可無不可。」

大師摯適齊,亞飯干適楚,三飯繚適蔡,四飯缺適秦。鼓方叔入於河,播鼗武入於漢,少師陽、擊磬襄,入於海。

逸民:伯夷、叔齐、虞仲、夷逸、朱张、柳下惠、少连。子曰:「不降其志,不辱其身,伯夷、叔齐与!」谓:「柳下惠、少连,降志辱身矣。言中伦,行中虑,其斯而已矣。」谓:「虞仲、夷逸,隐居放言。身中清,废中权。」「我则异于是,无可无不可。」

大师挚适齐,亚饭干适楚,三饭缭适蔡,四饭缺适秦。鼓方叔入于河,播鼗武入于汉,少师阳、击磬襄,入于海。

CHAP. VIII. 1. The men who have retired to privacy from the world have been Po-i, Shu-ch'i, Yu-chung, I-yi, Chu-chang, Hui of Liu-hsia, and Shao-lien. 2. The Master said, 'Refusing to surrender their wills, or to submit to any taint in their persons;— such, I think, were Po-i and Shu-ch'i. 3. 'It may be said of Hui of Liu-hsia, and of Shao-lien, that they surrendered their wills, and submitted to taint in their persons, but their words corresponded with reason, and their actions were such as men are anxious to see. This is all that is to be remarked in them. 4. 'It may be said of Yu-chung and I-yi, that, while they hid themselves in their seclusion, they gave a license to their words; but, in their persons, they succeeded in preserving their purity, and, in their retirement, they acted according to the exigency of the times. 5. 'I am different from all these. I have no course for which I am predetermined, and no course against which I am predetermined.'

CHAP. IX. 1. The grand music master, Chih, went to Ch'i. 2. Kan, the master of the band at the second meal, went to Ch'u. Liao, the band master at the third meal, went to Ts'ai. Chueh, the band master at the fourth meal, went to Ch'in. 3. Fang-shu, the drum master, withdrew to the north of the river. 4. Wu, the master of the hand drum, withdrew to the Han. 5. Yang, the assistant music master, and Hsiang, master of the musical stone, withdrew to an island in the sea.

SEAL SCRIPT

周公謂魯公曰：「君子不施其親，不使大臣怨乎不以。故舊無大故，則不棄也。無求備於一人。」

周有八士：伯達、伯適、仲突、仲忽、叔夜、叔夏、季隨、季騧。

周公谓鲁公曰：「君子不施其亲，不使大臣怨乎不以。故旧无大故，则不弃也。无求备于一人。」

周有八士：伯达、伯适、仲突、仲忽、叔夜、叔夏、季随、季騧。

CHAP. X. The duke of Chau addressed his son, the duke of Lu, saying, 'The virtuous prince does not neglect his relations. He does not cause the great ministers to repine at his not employing them. Without some great cause, he does not dismiss from their offices the members of old families. He does not seek in one man talents for every employment.'

CHAP. XI. To Chau belonged the eight officers, Po-ta, Po-kwo, Chung-tu, Chung-hwu, Shu-ya, Shu-hsia, Chi-sui, and Chi-kwa.

SEAL SCRIPT

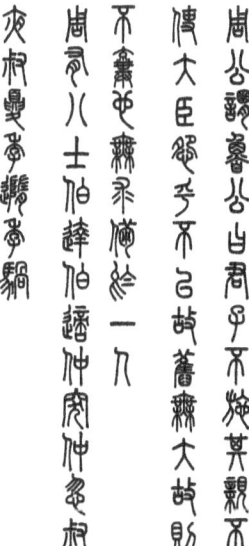

子張第十九

子張曰：「士見危致命，見得思義，祭思敬，喪思哀，其可已矣。」

子張曰：「執德不弘，信道不篤，焉能為有？焉能為亡？」

子夏之門人問交於子張。子張曰：「子夏云何？」對曰：「子夏曰：『可者與之，其不可者拒之。』」子張曰：「異乎吾所聞：君子尊賢而容眾，嘉善而矜不能。我之大賢與，於人何所不容？我之不賢與，人將拒我，如之何其拒人也？」

子张第十九

子张曰：「士见危致命，见得思义，祭思敬，丧思哀，其可已矣。」

子张曰：「执德不弘，信道不笃，焉能为有？焉能为亡？」

子夏之门人问交于子张。子张曰：「子夏云何？」对曰：「子夏曰：『可者与之，其不可者拒之。』」子张曰：「异乎吾所闻：君子尊贤而容众，嘉善而矜不能。我之大贤与，于人何所不容？我之不贤与，人将拒我，如之何其拒人也？」

BOOK XIX. TSZE-CHANG.

CHAP. I. Tsze-chang said, 'The scholar, trained for public duty, seeing threatening danger, is prepared to sacrifice his life. When the opportunity of gain is presented to him, he thinks of righteousness. In sacrificing, his thoughts are reverential. In mourning, his thoughts are about the grief which he should feel. Such a man commands our approbation indeed.'

CHAP. II. Tsze-chang said, 'When a man holds fast to virtue, but without seeking to enlarge it, and believes right principles, but without firm sincerity, what account can be made of his existence or non-existence?'

CHAP. III. The disciples of Tsze-hsia asked Tsze-chang about the principles that should characterize mutual intercourse. Tsze- chang asked, 'What does Tsze-hsia say on the subject?' They replied, 'Tsze-hsia says:— "Associate with those who can advantage you. Put away from you those who cannot do so."' Tsze-chang observed, 'This is different from what I have learned. The superior man honours the talented and virtuous, and bears with all. He praises the good, and pities the incompetent. Am I possessed of great talents and virtue?— who is there among men whom I will not bear with? Am I devoid of talents and virtue?— men will put me away from them. What have we to do with the putting away of others?'

SEAL SCRIPT

子夏曰：「雖小道，必有可觀者焉；致遠恐泥，是以君子不為也。」

子夏曰：「日知其所亡，月無忘其所能，可謂好學也已矣。」

子夏曰：「博學而篤志，切問而近思，仁在其中矣。」

子夏曰：「百工居肆以成其事，君子學以致其道。」

子夏曰：「小人之過也必文。」

子夏曰：「君子有三變：望之儼然，即之也溫，聽其言也厲。」

子夏曰：「虽小道，必有可观者焉；致远恐泥，是以君子不为也。」

子夏曰：「日知其所亡，月无忘其所能，可谓好学也已矣。」

子夏曰：「博学而笃志，切问而近思，仁在其中矣。」

子夏曰：「百工居肆以成其事，君子学以致其道。」

子夏曰：「小人之过也必文。」

子夏曰：「君子有三变：望之俨然，即之也温，听其言也厉。」

CHAP. IV. Tsze-hsia said, 'Even in inferior studies and employments there is something worth being looked at; but if it be attempted to carry them out to what is remote, there is a danger of their proving inapplicable. Therefore, the superior man does not practise them.'

CHAP. V. Tsze-hsia said, 'He, who from day to day recognises what he has not yet, and from month to month does not forget what he has attained to, may be said indeed to love to learn.'

CHAP. VI. Tsze-hsia said, 'There are learning extensively, and having a firm and sincere aim; inquiring with earnestness, and reflecting with self-application:— virtue is in such a course.'

CHAP. VII. Tsze-hsia said, 'Mechanics have their shops to dwell in, in order to accomplish their works. The superior man learns, in order to reach to the utmost of his principles.'

CHAP. VIII. Tsze-hsia said, 'The mean man is sure to gloss his faults.'

CHAP. IX. Tsze-hsia said, 'The superior man undergoes three changes. Looked at from a distance, he appears stern; when approached, he is mild; when he is heard to speak, his language is firm and decided.'

SEAL SCRIPT

　　子夏曰：「君子信而後勞其民，未信則以為厲己也；信而後諫，未信則以為謗己也。」

　　子夏曰：「大德不踰閑，小德出入可也。」

　　子游曰：「子夏之門人小子，當洒掃、應對、進退，則可矣。抑末也，本之則無。如之何？」子夏聞之曰：「噫！言游過矣！君子之道，孰先傳焉？孰後倦焉？譬諸草木，區以別矣。君子之道，焉可誣也？有始有卒者，其惟聖人乎！」

　　子夏曰：「君子信而后劳其民，未信则以为厉己也；信而后谏，未信则以为谤己也。」

　　子夏曰：「大德不逾闲，小德出入可也。」

　　子游曰：「子夏之门人小子，当洒扫、应对、进退，则可矣。抑末也，本之则无。如之何？」子夏闻之曰：「噫！言游过矣！君子之道，孰先传焉？孰后倦焉？譬诸草木，区以别矣。君子之道，焉可诬也？有始有卒者，其惟圣人乎！」

CHAP. X. Tsze-hsia said, 'The superior man, having obtained their confidence, may then impose labours on his people. If he have not gained their confidence, they will think that he is oppressing them. Having obtained the confidence of his prince, one may then remonstrate with him. If he have not gained his confidence, the prince will think that he is vilifying him.'

CHAP. XI. Tsze-hsia said, 'When a person does not transgress the boundary line in the great virtues, he may pass and repass it in the small virtues.'

CHAP. XII. 1. Tsze-yu said, 'The disciples and followers of Tsze-hsia, in sprinkling and sweeping the ground, in answering and replying, in advancing and receding, are sufficiently accomplished. But these are only the branches of learning, and they are left ignorant of what is essential.— How can they be acknowledged as sufficiently taught?' 2. Tsze-hsia heard of the remark and said, 'Alas! Yen Yu is wrong. According to the way of the superior man in teaching, what departments are there which he considers of prime importance, and delivers? what are there which he considers of secondary importance, and allows himself to be idle about? But as in the case of plants, which are assorted according to their classes, so he deals with his disciples. How can the way of a superior man be such as to make fools of any of them? Is it not the sage alone, who can unite in one the beginning and the consummation of learning?'

SEAL SCRIPT

子夏曰：「仕而優則學，學而優則仕。」

子游曰：「喪致乎哀而止。」

子游曰：「吾友張也，為難能也。然而未仁。」

曾子曰：「堂堂乎張也，難與並為仁矣。」

曾子曰：「吾聞諸夫子：人未有自致者也，必也親喪乎！」

曾子曰：「吾聞諸夫子：孟莊子之孝也，其他可能也；其不改父之臣，與父之政，是難能也。」

子夏曰：「仕而优则学，学而优则仕。」

子游曰：「丧致乎哀而止。」

子游曰：「吾友张也，为难能也。然而未仁。」

曾子曰：「堂堂乎张也，难与并为仁矣。」

曾子曰：「吾闻诸夫子：人未有自致者也，必也亲丧乎！」

曾子曰：「吾闻诸夫子：孟庄子之孝也，其他可能也；其不改父之臣，与父之政，是难能也。」

CHAP. XIII. Tsze-hsia said, 'The officer, having discharged all his duties, should devote his leisure to learning. The student, having completed his learning, should apply himself to be an officer.'

CHAP. XIV. Tsze-hsia said, 'Mourning, having been carried to the utmost degree of grief, should stop with that.'

CHAP. XV. Tsze-hsia said, 'My friend Chang can do things which are hard to be done, but yet he is not perfectly virtuous.'

CHAP. XVI. The philosopher Tsang said, 'How imposing is the manner of Chang! It is difficult along with him to practise virtue.'

CHAP. XVII. The philosopher Tsang said, 'I heard this from our Master:— "Men may not have shown what is in them to the full extent, and yet they will be found to do so, on occasion of mourning for their parents."'

CHAP. XVIII. The philosopher Tsang said, 'I have heard this from our Master:— "The filial piety of Mang Chwang, in other matters, was what other men are competent to, but, as seen in his not changing the ministers of his father, nor his father's mode of government, it is difficult to be attained to."'

SEAL SCRIPT

　　孟氏使陽膚為士師，問於曾子。曾子曰：「上失其道，民散久矣。如得其情，則哀矜而勿喜。」

　　子貢曰：「紂之不善，不如是之甚也。是以君子惡居下流，天下之惡皆歸焉。」

　　子貢曰：「君子之過也，如日月之食焉：過也，人皆見之；更也，人皆仰之。」

　　衛公孫朝問於子貢曰：「仲尼焉學？」子貢曰：「文武之道，未墜於地，在人。賢者識其大者，不賢者識其小者，莫不有文武之道焉。夫子焉不學？而亦何常師之有？」

　　孟氏使阳肤为士师，问于曾子。曾子曰：「上失其道，民散久矣。如得其情，则哀矜而勿喜。」

　　子贡曰：「纣之不善，不如是之甚也。是以君子恶居下流，天下之恶皆归焉。」

　　子贡曰：「君子之过也，如日月之食焉：过也，人皆见之；更也，人皆仰之。」

　　卫公孙朝问于子贡曰：「仲尼焉学？」子贡曰：「文武之道，未坠于地，在人。贤者识其大者，不贤者识其小者，莫不有文武之道焉。夫子焉不学？而亦何常师之有？」

CHAP. XIX. The chief of the Mang family having appointed Yang Fu to be chief criminal judge, the latter consulted the philosopher Tsang. Tsang said, 'The rulers have failed in their duties, and the people consequently have been disorganised, for a long time. When you have found out the truth of any accusation, be grieved for and pity them, and do not feel joy at your own ability.'

CHAP. XX. Tsze-kung said, 'Chau's wickedness was not so great as that name implies. Therefore, the superior man hates to dwell in a low-lying situation, where all the evil of the world will flow in upon him.'

CHAP. XXI. Tsze-kung said, 'The faults of the superior man are like the eclipses of the sun and moon. He has his faults, and all men see them; he changes again, and all men look up to him.'

CHAP. XXII. 1. Kung-sun Ch'ao of Wei asked Tsze-kung, saying, 'From whom did Chung-ni get his learning?' 2. Tsze-kung replied, 'The doctrines of Wan and Wu have not yet fallen to the ground. They are to be found among men. Men of talents and virtue remember the greater principles of them, and others, not possessing such talents and virtue, remember the smaller. Thus, all possess the doctrines of Wan and Wu. Where could our Master go that he should not have an opportunity of learning them? And yet what necessity was there for his having a regular master?'

SEAL SCRIPT

　　叔孫武叔語大夫於朝，曰：「子貢賢於仲尼。」子服景伯以告子貢。子貢曰：「譬之宮牆，賜之牆也及肩，窺見室家之好。夫子之牆數仞，不得其門而入，不見宗廟之美，百官之富。得其門者或寡矣。夫子之云，不亦宜乎！」

　　叔孫武叔毀仲尼。子貢曰：「無以為也，仲尼不可毀也。他人之賢者，丘陵也，猶可踰也；仲尼，日月也，無得而踰焉。人雖欲自絕，其何傷於日月乎？多見其不知量也！」

　　叔孙武叔语大夫于朝，曰：「子贡贤于仲尼。」子服景伯以告子贡。子贡曰：「譬之宫墙，赐之墙也及肩，窥见室家之好。夫子之墙数仞，不得其门而入，不见宗庙之美，百官之富。得其门者或寡矣。夫子之云，不亦宜乎！」

　　叔孙武叔毁仲尼。子贡曰：「无以为也，仲尼不可毁也。他人之贤者，丘陵也，犹可逾也；仲尼，日月也，无得而逾焉。人虽欲自绝，其何伤于日月乎？多见其不知量也！」

CHAP. XXIII. 1. Shu-sun Wu-shu observed to the great officers in the court, saying, 'Tsze-kung is superior to Chung-ni.' 2. Tsze-fu Ching-po reported the observation to Tsze-kung, who said, 'Let me use the comparison of a house and its encompassing wall. My wall only reaches to the shoulders. One may peep over it, and see whatever is valuable in the apartments. 3. 'The wall of my Master is several fathoms high. If one do not find the door and enter by it, he cannot see the ancestral temple with its beauties, nor all the officers in their rich array. 4. 'But I may assume that they are few who find the door. Was not the observation of the chief only what might have been expected?'

CHAP. XXIV. Shu-sun Wu-shu having spoken revilingly of Chung-ni, Tsze-kung said, 'It is of no use doing so. Chung-ni cannot be reviled. The talents and virtue of other men are hillocks and mounds which may be stepped over. Chung-ni is the sun or moon, which it is not possible to step over. Although a man may wish to cut himself off from the sage, what harm can he do to the sun or moon? He only shows that he does not know his own capacity.

SEAL SCRIPT

275

陳子禽謂子貢曰:「子為恭也,仲尼豈賢於子乎?」子貢曰:「君子一言以為知,一言以為不知,言不可不慎也。夫子之不可及也,猶天之不可階而升也。夫子之得邦家者,所謂立之斯立,道之斯行,綏之斯來,動之斯和。其生也榮,其死也哀,如之何其可及也。」

陈子禽谓子贡曰:「子为恭也,仲尼岂贤于子乎?」子贡曰:「君子一言以为知,一言以为不知,言不可不慎也。夫子之不可及也,犹天之不可阶而升也。夫子之得邦家者,所谓立之斯立,道之斯行,绥之斯来,动之斯和。其生也荣,其死也哀,如之何其可及也。」

CHAP. XXV. 1. Ch'an Tsze-ch'in, addressing Tsze-kung, said, 'You are too modest. How can Chung-ni be said to be superior to you?' 2. Tsze-kung said to him, 'For one word a man is often deemed to be wise, and for one word he is often deemed to be foolish. We ought to be careful indeed in what we say. 3. 'Our Master cannot be attained to, just in the same way as the heavens cannot be gone up to by the steps of a stair. 4. 'Were our Master in the position of the ruler of a State or the chief of a Family, we should find verified the description which has been given of a sage's rule:— he would plant the people, and forthwith they would be established; he would lead them on, and forthwith they would follow him; he would make them happy, and forthwith multitudes would resort to his dominions; he would stimulate them, and forthwith they would be harmonious. While he lived, he would be glorious. When he died, he would be bitterly lamented. How is it possible for him to be attained to?'

SEAL SCRIPT

堯曰第二十

堯曰：「咨！爾舜！天之曆數在爾躬。允執其中。四海困窮，天祿永終。」舜亦以命禹。曰：「予小子履，敢用玄牡，敢昭告于皇皇后帝：有罪不敢赦。帝臣不蔽，簡在帝心。朕躬有罪，無以萬方；萬方有罪，罪在朕躬。」周有大賚，善人是富。「雖有周親，不如仁人。百姓有過，在予一人。」謹權量，審法度，修廢官，四方之政行焉。興滅國，繼絕世，舉逸民，天下之民歸心焉。所重：民、食、喪、祭。寬則得眾，信則民任焉，敏則有功，公則說。

尧曰第二十

尧曰：「咨！尔舜！天之历数在尔躬。允执其中。四海困穷，天禄永终。」舜亦以命禹。曰：「予小子履，敢用玄牡，敢昭告于皇皇后帝：有罪不敢赦。帝臣不蔽，简在帝心。朕躬有罪，无以万方；万方有罪，罪在朕躬。」周有大赉，善人是富。「虽有周亲，不如仁人。百姓有过，在予一人。」谨权量，审法度，修废官，四方之政行焉。兴灭国，继绝世，举逸民，天下之民归心焉。所重：民、食、丧、祭。宽则得众，信则民任焉，敏则有功，公则说。

BOOK XX. YAO YUEH.

CHAP. I. 1. Yao said, 'Oh! you, Shun, the Heaven-determined order of succession now rests in your person. Sincerely hold fast the due Mean. If there shall be distress and want within the four seas, the Heavenly revenue will come to a perpetual end.' 2. Shun also used the same language in giving charge to Yu. 3. T'ang said, 'I the child Li, presume to use a dark-coloured victim, and presume to announce to Thee, O most great and sovereign God, that the sinner I dare not pardon, and thy ministers, O God, I do not keep in obscurity. The examination of them is by thy mind, O God. If, in my person, I commit offences, they are not to be attributed to you, the people of the myriad regions. If you in the myriad regions commit offences, these offences must rest on my person.' 4. Chau conferred great gifts, and the good were enriched. 5. 'Although he has his near relatives, they are not equal to my virtuous men. The people are throwing blame upon me, the One man.' 6. He carefully attended to the weights and measures, examined the body of the laws, restored the discarded officers, and the good government of the kingdom took its course. 7. He revived States that had been extinguished, restored families whose line of succession had been broken, and called to office those who had retired into obscurity, so that throughout the kingdom the hearts of the people turned towards him. 8. What he attached chief importance to, were the food of the people, the duties of mourning, and sacrifices. 9. By his generosity, he won all. By his sincerity, he made the people repose trust in him. By his earnest activity, his achievements were great. By his justice, all were delighted.

SEAL SCRIPT

堯曰第二十

堯曰咨爾舜天之曆數在爾躬

允執其中四海困窮天祿永終

舜亦以命禹曰予小子履敢用玄牡

敢昭告于皇皇后帝有罪不敢赦

帝臣不蔽簡在帝心朕躬有罪無以萬方

萬方有罪罪在朕躬周有大賚善人是富

雖有周親不如仁人百姓有過在予一人

謹權量審法度修廢官四方之政行焉

興滅國繼絕世舉逸民天下之民歸心焉

所重民食喪祭寬則得眾信則民任焉

敏則有功公則說

　　子張問於孔子曰：「何如斯可以從政矣？」子曰：「尊五美，屏四惡，斯可以從政矣。」子張曰：「何謂五美？」子曰：「君子惠而不費，勞而不怨，欲而不貪，泰而不驕，威而不猛。」子張曰：「何謂惠而不費？」子曰：「因民之所利而利之，斯不亦惠而不費乎？擇可勞而勞之，又誰怨？欲仁而得仁，又焉貪？君子無眾寡，無小大，無敢慢，斯不亦泰而不驕乎？君子正其衣冠，尊其瞻視，儼然人望而畏之，斯不亦威而不猛乎？」子張曰：「何謂四惡？」子曰：「不教而殺謂之虐；不戒視成謂之暴；慢令致期謂之賊；猶之與人也，出納之吝，謂之有司。」

　　子张问于孔子曰：「何如斯可以从政矣？」子曰：「尊五美，屏四恶，斯可以从政矣。」子张曰：「何谓五美？」子曰：「君子惠而不费，劳而不怨，欲而不贪，泰而不骄，威而不猛。」子张曰：「何谓惠而不费？」子曰：「因民之所利而利之，斯不亦惠而不费乎？择可劳而劳之，又谁怨？欲仁而得仁，又焉贪？君子无众寡，无小大，无敢慢，斯不亦泰而不骄乎？君子正其衣冠，尊其瞻视，俨然人望而畏之，斯不亦威而不猛乎？」子张曰：「何谓四恶？」子曰：「不教而杀谓之虐；不戒视成谓之暴；慢令致期谓之贼；犹之与人也，出纳之吝，谓之有司。」

CHAP. II. 1. Tsze-chang asked Confucius, saying, 'In what way should a person in authority act in order that he may conduct government properly?' The Master replied, 'Let him honour the five excellent, and banish away the four bad, things;— then may he conduct government properly.' Tsze-chang said, 'What are meant by the five excellent things?' The Master said, 'When the person in authority is beneficent without great expenditure; when he lays tasks on the people without their repining; when he pursues what he desires without being covetous; when he maintains a dignified ease without being proud; when he is majestic without being fierce.' 2. Tsze-chang said, 'What is meant by being beneficent without great expenditure?' The Master replied, 'When the person in authority makes more beneficial to the people the things from which they naturally derive benefit;— is not this being beneficent without great expenditure? When he chooses the labours which are proper, and makes them labour on them, who will repine? When his desires are set on benevolent government, and he secures it, who will accuse him of covetousness? Whether he has to do with many people or few, or with things great or small, he does not dare to indicate any disrespect;— is not this to maintain a dignified ease without any pride? He adjusts his clothes and cap, and throws a dignity into his looks, so that, thus dignified, he is looked at with awe;— is not this to be majestic without being fierce?' 3. Tsze-chang then asked, 'What are meant by the four bad things?' The Master said, 'To put

SEAL SCRIPT

子曰:「不知命,無以為君子也。不知禮,無以立也。不知言,無以知人也。」

子曰:「不知命,无以为君子也。不知礼,无以立也。不知言,无以知人也。」

the people to death without having instructed them;— this is called cruelty. To require from them, suddenly, the full tale of work, without having given them warning;— this is called oppression. To issue orders as if without urgency, at first, and, when the time comes, to insist on them with severity;— this is called injury. And, generally, in the giving pay or rewards to men, to do it in a stingy way;— this is called acting the part of a mere official.'

CHAP III. 1. The Master said, 'Without recognising the ordinances of Heaven, it is impossible to be a superior man. 2. 'Without an acquaintance with the rules of Propriety, it is impossible for the character to be established. 3. 'Without knowing the force of words, it is impossible to know men.'

SEAL SCRIPT

DISCOVER MORE ANCIENT WISDOM

We invite you to discover two treasures of ancient Chinese wisdom.

"Tao Te Ching" by Lao Tzu
Ultimate Bilingual Edition (4-in-1)
Lao Tzu reflects on the Way—how to live with ease, act without strain, and find strength in simplicity. Short lines, long insight.

"The Art of War" by Sun Tzu
Ultimate Bilingual Edition (4-in-1)
Sun Tzu teaches timing, terrain, deception, and preparation—how to read a situation before it unfolds and win with minimal cost. One page can change how you plan, negotiate, and decide.

Join thousands of readers who return to these pages again and again. Find your copies at major online bookstores worldwide.